PRAISE FOR
It's Time to Give a FECK

"THIS BOOK DOESN'T just advocate for decency—it exudes it. If we all followed Chaz Ebert's lead, the world would be a more caring place."

—Adam Grant
#1 New York Times Bestselling Author
of *Hidden Potential* and *Think Again*

"IN *IT'S TIME TO GIVE A FECK*, Chaz Ebert describes how to capture our best instincts as people and turn them into a healthy way of living. I hope that everyone has a chance to read it, and most importantly, to live its principles."

—Chris Kelly
Co-owner of the Sacramento Kings;
Former Chief Privacy Officer,
General Counsel, and Head of
Global Public Policy at Facebook

"WE ALL HOLD THE ABILITY to transform empathy into action for greater, more positive personal and global impact. With her words of wisdom, Chaz Ebert has beautifully showcased just how each of us can put this potential into action and, through our service to others, always keep hope alive."

—Reverend Jesse L. Jackson Sr.
Founder and President of the Rainbow PUSH Coalition

"HUMANITY DOESN'T NEED complexity to solve our problems; we simply need to return to the undeniable power of forgiveness, empathy, compassion, and kindness. Inside, Chaz Ebert shows us just how."

—Emma Seppälä, PhD
Yale Lecturer and Author of
The Happiness Track and *Sovereign*

"BRAVO, CHAZ EBERT, for rising to the occasion to share such an incredibly hopeful and realistic perspective on goodness in our world!"

—Lawrence Bender, Producer
Inglourious Basterds, Pulp Fiction, Good Will Hunting,
and more—films with 37 Academy Award
nominations and 9 wins

"A WARM, ARTICULATE display about the powerful potential of universally shared human values."

—Verdine White
6-Time Grammy-Winning Artist,
Rock and Roll Hall of Fame Inductee,
and Founding Member of Earth, Wind & Fire

"CHAZ EBERT IS tipping the scales on moving humanity to a better place. *It's Time to Give a FECK* (Forgiveness, Empathy, Compassion, and Kindness) is Chaz Ebert's first-hand journey into what the world needs now more than ever, including a Department of Peace!"

—Andrew Davis
Director of *The Fugitive*, *Holes*, and *The Guardian*

"CHAZ EBERT HAS simplified and made practical the principles of forgiveness, empathy, compassion, and kindness. She has also tied them together in a way where they become an undeniable formula for global unity—something we need more than ever right now."

—Susan Buffett
Chair of the Susan Thompson Buffett Foundation

"AS I READ THROUGH *It's Time to Give a FECK*, I was chuckling to myself thinking, *Yup that's pretty much all we need to know right here, skillfully and delightfully presented*."

—FREDERIC LUSKIN, PhD, Director of the Stanford Forgiveness Project and Author of *Forgive for Good*

"IN A WORLD INCREASINGLY divided and violent, as Chaz Ebert so powerfully puts forward in her new book, empathy and compassion are the only ways forward to save us from ourselves. It's time to give a FECK!"

—GREGORY NAVA, Academy Award-Nominated Screenwriter of *El Norte*, Director of *Selena* and *Mi Familia*

"WE ALL HAVE WITHIN ourselves a fountain of healing for the world. In *It's Time to Give a FECK*, Chaz Ebert ushers forward a new paradigm of hope by opening our hearts and inviting us to lead ourselves into a better future of love-inspired action."

—E. ELISABET LAHTI, Ph.D.
Founder of Sisu Lab and Author of
Gentle Power: A Revolution in How We Think, Lead, and Succeed Using the Finnish Art of Sisu

"I CAN'T IMAGINE a better person than Chaz Ebert to write a book about generosity of spirit. In a time of growing cynicism, polarization, and indifference, she takes the reader on an aspirational journey that is personal as well as collective. From its first pages—in which she invokes her sorely missed husband, 'Roger took his "leave of presence," as he called it'—Chaz makes a persuasive case for empathetic engagement."

—Annette Insdorf
Columbia University Film Professor
and Author of *Indelible Shadows: Film and the Holocaust*

"*IT'S TIME TO GIVE A FECK* shows us how to step into the shoes of others and discover the shared humanity that binds us all. Chaz's compassionate exploration of empathy is not just intellectually stimulating, it's deeply moving. It will challenge your assumptions, open your heart, and leave you yearning for a more understanding world."

—Cortney Kane Sides
Psychic Medium, International Speaker,
Author, and Host of *Cosmically Connected with Cortney Kane Sides* Podcast

"INCREDIBLE! CHAZ HAS read my past, present, and future mind and created a monumental work. In this book, you will discover my many minds about the need to bring more compassion and goodness into the world."

—DEBORAH SZEKELY
Godmother of Health and Fitness
and Founder of Rancho La Puerta
and The Golden Door Health Spas

"IT'S TIME TO GIVE A FECK . . . now! Chaz Ebert's timely, insightful, and much-needed book breaks down concepts that are not new to us, while heightening our awareness and viability of these principles and values. It's my new go-to book for inspiration in creating a more meaningful and conscience life for me and others."

—MARLENE MCGUIRT
Director of Development of
WeSPARK Cancer Support Center

"OUR WORLD TODAY has become unrecognizable to most thoughtful and decent people. *It's Time to Give a FECK* is a gift to mankind that seeks to *unite* all people around a thoughtful combination of guiding principles and actions. I salute my dear friend's artful and timely masterpiece, which comes to us at the perfect defining moment."

—LOU WEISBACH
National Political and Business Leader
and Cofounder of the American
Center for Cures

IT'S TIME TO GIVE A

FECK

IT'S TIME TO GIVE A FECK

ELEVATING HUMANITY THROUGH FORGIVENESS, EMPATHY, COMPASSION, AND KINDNESS

CHAZ EBERT

It's Time to Give a FECK: Elevating Humanity through Forgiveness, Empathy, Compassion, and Kindness

Published by Forefront Books, Nashville, Tennessee.
Distributed by Simon & Schuster.
Library of Congress Control Number: 2024901362

Print ISBN: 978-1-63763-247-5
E-book ISBN: 978-1-63763-248-2

Cover Design by Molly von Borstel, Faceout Studio
Interior Design by Mary Susan Oleson, Blu Design Concepts

Printed in the United States of America

TABLE of CONTENTS

THE FECK PRINCIPLES

FECK PRINCIPLE 1: *Forgiveness*

FECK PRINCIPLE 2: *Empathy*

FECK PRINCIPLE 3: *Compassion*

FECK PRINCIPLE 4: *Kindness*

To Roger, whose capacity
for empathy knew no bounds.
And to the universal source of love
that binds us all together.

Acknowledgments

FIRST, to my family, whose kindness and compassion I want to pay forward—*thank you!*

To my mother, Mrs. Johnnie Mae Hammel, who brought so much sunshine into our lives and showed us unconditional love.

To my father, Mr. Wiley J. Hammel, who provided for us and made us feel secure and grateful.

To my sisters, Carrie, Martha, Adele, and Donna, who taught me the meaning of girl power and female solidarity.

To my brothers, Johnnie, Wiley, Sam, and Andre, who taught me that boys and girls can be friends and equals. And to my heavenly brothers, George and Baby, whose presence I feel even though I never met them on this earth. Thank you.

SECOND, to those kind souls who surrounded me during this journey:

ACKNOWLEDGMENTS

Thank you to Joscelyn Duffy, who labored through each reworking of this book with me, supporting me at every step until this final product was achieved. Joscelyn, thank you for telling me that there was a place for these principles in the world. Without your support and counsel, I truly would not have made it to the finish line!

To my daughter, Sonia Evans, and my son, Josibiah Smith, to Daniel Jackson and Matt Fagerholm of Rogerebert.com, and to Chris Lautenslager, who all so generously read versions of the book. *Thank you* for cheering me on, and especially for urging me not to abandon the book when I was faltering. Your empathy meant everything to me. To Kia Harris of Forefront Books, thank you for your insight and guidance.

And to all in my life and in this world who through your examples taught me that forgiveness, empathy, compassion, and kindness can indeed change the world for the better—*thank you!*

Foreword

LONG BEFORE the days of my becoming the first Black woman to host the *TODAY* show or premiering the *Tamron Hall Show*, I landed on Chicago's doorstep. It was August 31, 1997, and I had just accepted a role as reporter with the Fox News station *WFLD*, directly on the Magnificent Mile, in the heart of city. I was twenty-seven years old and swimming in fear. Outside of the brief in-and-out interview to secure the role, I had never been to the city and didn't have a single personal acquaintance there. Since college, I had been happily working as a reporter in my hometown of Dallas–Fort Worth—a place where I was assured to always be surrounded by the love of friends and family. My parents had seen me off at the Dallas airport that morning. Everything about arriving in Chicago frightened me, as I stood there carrying my single suitcase and the cage that held my cherished cockatiel bird.

On the ride from the airport, my taxi driver asked me why I was in Chicago. I told him I had moved there to be a reporter. "Good luck! It's a tough town," he said begrudgingly. He then added that I should expect to gain a lot of weight and drink a lot. There I was, the wheels of the taxi moving me forward on my journey yet feeling frozen by the utter fright that things would not work out. Then news of Princess Diana's death rushed across the airwaves and was enough to push me straight over the edge. I felt total regret for having made the decision to move to Chicago.

In an attempt to glue my two feet firmly in place, I remembered what a dear friend and fellow member of the National Association of Black Journalists had told me when he said I should take the job there. "Chicago is going to make you a new star," he had so confidently expressed. It was a "news town" and a place that supported Black women and journalists. Oprah Winfrey called the city home as did Allison Payne, Diann Burns, and Robin Robinson—iconic Black female newspeople who were known around the country—were all making their mark there. Why not me?

The fear of failing in the Windy City had not left me, yet I tried to keep the faith as I dove into my first few weeks of my new role. At lunch, I would sometimes wander around the Magnificent Mile and frequent the food court at the Water Tower building on Michigan Avenue—a place that took on a whole new meaning to me one Tuesday. While grabbing a quick bite, I could feel the stare of a Black woman behind the counter checking me out. She then propped up and said, "You're the new Black girl on Fox 32."

"I am," I said.

"Oh, we're watching!" she enthusiastically replied with a kindness and ownership that left me feeling as though a loved one had reached out to embrace me in the biggest way possible. Like the radiant North Star, this human being had gifted me the most beautiful act of kindness and hope. It gave me the confidence I needed to stay in Chicago.

Within a matter of months, I had started to build a reputation in town. When a controversial decision by the WFLD news director led to the firing of the anchor for *Fox News in the Morning* I was offered the role. The move from reporter to anchor should have been a cherished time in my career, but it felt tainted by the fact that someone had to be cut to make room for me to advance. Yet another joyous moment was crushed, just like the taxi driver's stark warning about Chicago being a tough town the day I had set foot in the city. If that wasn't enough to weigh heavily on my heart, a local reporter then referred to me as a Halle Berry look-alike. Any acts of kindness I had experienced since landing in Chicago felt immediately erased by that one powerful moment of rejection and for not being seen for who I was. Maybe it was time for me to go back home to Texas.

It was then that an unexpected invitation arrived to join Chaz and Roger Ebert for a Fourth of July gathering at their summer house just outside New Buffalo, Michigan. Over my entire career, I had watched Roger Ebert and WGN, and *Siskel & Ebert* had become a hallmark of what Chicago meant to me. I was convinced that Chaz and Roger must had made a mistake and mixed my name up with someone else's. I had only met them once, walking into a movie screening at Lake Street Screening Room off Michigan Avenue. There was no way they knew who I was.

Regardless, like a sleuth following up on a good lead, I decided to brave the unknown and make the hour-long drive to the wooded beauty of Harbert where I arrived at their brick Tudor home, seated squarely on the bluffs of Lake Michigan. There were parked cars for miles, an outdoor bandstand with hopping Motown music enlivening those on the dance floor, and a crowd easily topping three hundred guests. Like the day I had set foot outside O'Hare Airport to mark Chicago as my new home, I felt completely overwhelmed. First stop: the washroom to collect my thoughts. What I didn't expect was what I would find within its walls.

On the washroom counter sat two figurines: one of a Black woman and one of a white man. "I'm their child! If they had a baby, it could be me!" I thought to myself about Chaz and Roger. Those two little porcelain creations gave me enough of the feeling of support I needed to go out and confidently be with everyone. It is difficult to fully explain that sudden wave of assurance, though as I walked out and witnessed Chaz being the most gracious host, it all made sense. There she was, walking around, making everyone feel seen and cared for. From her, I felt an overwhelming sense of welcome and kindness. What amazed me most was that from a city known to be a hard-news town, Chaz and Roger had brought together people from the *Chicago Sun-Times*, the *Tribune*, ABC, CBS, NBC, WGN, and Fox, along with countless local writers, filmmakers, and friends. And everyone seemed to be having a grand time.

Doing my best to inconspicuously blend in, I said hello to familiar faces as Chaz made sure I was introduced to those I didn't know. Then I saw him—the writer who had called me a Halle Berry look-alike. My heart sank yet again. Had I not felt frozen in the moment, I might just have run. Then Roger spoke directly to him. "No one wants to be compared to anyone else. That's not fair," he said. It was a single act of loving support so powerful that left me feeling as though my newfound "parents" were rooting for me. I felt tougher and very much at home as that defining moment made me recognize that the good things that were happening to me were meant for me to pass along good things to other people. It became a critical turning point in my decision to stay in Chicago. Up until then, the high moment of my career success of becoming an anchor had felt hollow, yet in a miraculous instant, that hole was filled with true unconditional compassion and love. Because of Chaz and Roger, I felt reinvigorated and more purposeful about moving forward spreading what was given to me—and I went on to brush off naysayers and not allow negativity to outshine the joy that people give us.

Years after being invited to their cookout and further forging our bond, I ran into Chaz and Roger at a newsstand at O'Hare International Airport—the place where it had all begun for me. Life had changed for them in many ways, and Roger was in a wheelchair. Despite his struggle to articulate himself and few words being said, not a bit of the kind compassion they had always offered me had faded. Once again, they embraced me so warmly that made it abundantly clear that my "parents" were still rooting for me.

This story is not my journey alone. It is so important that we all embrace and expand the conversation about the magical moments where others make the choice to extend the shining lights of forgiveness, empathy, compassion, and kindness—the FECK Principles. The tradition of joy, love, and support will never go out of style, but we all have to be active participants. That's what Chaz is welcoming us to do in *It's Time to Give a FECK.*

Because of Chaz, I have experienced first-hand why any of us should dive in and embrace the perspective on how good our world can be. From the day we met, she has reminded me of the strong women who had raised me—my mother, her friends, my aunts. Their outpouring of care and kindness has always left me feeling so at home and I can only hope that each of us has the opportunity to encounter people like Chaz or that angelic woman from my early-Chicago days at the food court—those who have undeniably made these principles a daily practice and who are constantly reminding us that none of us has to go it alone.

TAMRON HALL

Emmy Award–winning journalist
and host of the *Tamron Hall Show*

In the Name of Love

TWENTY-FOUR. That is the number of years I shared with Roger Ebert and the number of years that motivated my very personal, deep-seated connection to empathy. Together, Roger and I experienced film, family, friends, the world, life, and death. He was one of the kindest and most thoughtful people I have ever met—a community builder who believed that movies are the most powerful "empathy-generating machine" in all the arts. "They let us understand hopes, aspirations, dreams, and fears," he would say. And when Roger had an idea, you could not steer him away from it until that idea was actualized. As a couple, we built a life upon the foundation of being advocates for empathy—for not "otherizing" those different from us, but rather understanding and recognizing everyone as a fellow traveler on this life journey. Professionally, we worked to encourage programs where empathy could be taught or experienced through cinema. Personally, we fostered empathy in our family through travel and introducing our grandchildren to various countries and cultures so they could be exposed to different peoples, languages, foods, and customs. We rallied around goodness, working to shine the light on those who possess and inspire in others empathy, compassion, and courage. Our lives ultimately came down to creating a greater discussion around these topics.

In early 2013, we began filming *Life Itself*, the documentary about Roger's life's work. Initially, Roger wondered why anyone would want to make a movie about a film critic. He had already turned down two proposals. Then, in December 2012, Steve James, director of the game-changing documentary *Hoop Dreams*, came to our Chicago home to meet with us and discuss his vision for Roger's story. Roger acquiesced when he learned that the team consisted of Emmy-nominated producer Garrett Basch, who had recommended Roger's memoir by the same title to filmmaker Steven Zaillian (Oscar winner for Best Adapted Screenplay for *Schindler's List*), who then recommended it to Martin Scorsese (*Raging Bull*,

Goodfellas, and the Oscar-winning director of *The Departed*). "How can we go wrong?" Roger reasoned when Steve James and his team made him an offer he could not refuse.

Having committed to the project, Roger made it clear that he wanted his documentary to be much more than the story of a film critic. But we definitely did not know it was going to be the version of *Life Itself* we ended up creating. When planning the film, Steve James originally thought he would be showing Roger in myriad situations: teaching and giving speeches, going to the movies and interviewing filmmakers, writing books, hosting dinner parties at our home in the country, traveling with family or to film festivals, and living his life doing such things as going to the opera, where, by the way, we had our first date. When we started filming, we thought Roger had many more years to live. Roger had been diagnosed with thyroid and salivary cancer in 2002 but had been successfully treated, and his cancer was in remission. The catastrophic effects of proton radiation after the return of his cancer in 2006 had caused him to lose his ability to speak and eat (except via a feeding tube), though he continued to write, teach, and travel. Roger had always been a man who loved to talk, tell jokes, and experience food with much gusto. He now wanted to use this movie to throw open the curtains and let the world see how it is for so many others living with disabilities in a similar situation—those who perhaps didn't have the platform to do so. He also wanted to create a film that would help spur empathy for filmmakers who may not have been given a fair break in the industry particularly because of their race or gender.

The day after we met with Steve James to begin filming, things took an unexpected turn. Roger fell and broke his hip as a result of medication that had the side effect of weakening his bones, initiating a new series of hospitalizations. It was during one of those hospital visits that we learned his cancer had returned, bringing with it a challenging battle. Roger remained steadfast in his vision and commitment to let Steve and the world in. "I don't want a movie made of my life that I wouldn't want to watch," he said. In other words, his story had to be honest and transparent, showing the man, warts and all, and not just the icon. He allowed Steve to film him in the hospital, providing a close-up perspective of his fight against cancer and its debilitating consequences. Steve would periodically bring Roger clips of the film to watch. They gave him hope, and in return, he gave Steve permission to continue with the film in whatever way he could. From that day, *Life Itself* became, among other things, an unflinchingly honest portrait of a painful reality.

I was initially against Roger showing the world so much of his journey. It seemed too personal and too painful. I wanted to protect him, but Roger was firm in his resolve. In hindsight, Roger's decision was the right one. Everything he did was true to who he was at the core. He was fearless, bringing forth a new level of candor, showing the viewer ground zero of the human body. He did it because he believed in showcasing the truth of the situation and he wanted to use the film to connect with others on an even deeper level. Roger accomplished all that he had envisioned. Upon the movie's release came a rush of letters, emails, and social media comments from others saying that the film had helped them by showing Roger's humanity through his vulnerability. They said that because he was open about how he was living with his illness, the line of demarcation between Roger and the viewer vanished.

Suddenly there was no great differentiation between either of them. In the end, Roger and the team of filmmakers had contributed in the greatest way they could to the "empathy machine" Roger had always believed movies to be.

Roger did not live long enough to see the completed version of *Life Itself*. He made his premature transition from this earth on April 4, 2013. From the time his cancer returned in 2006 until that fateful day in 2013 when I had to let him go, I remained so impressed with his courage and his determination to live a meaningful life. I didn't want to pity him or feel sorry for him, and he didn't want sympathy. Instead, I wanted to empathize with him in the deep way he did for others. As we made our way through cancer together, I was so grateful to the doctors and nurses and the home care staff who helped to make his last seven years so full and beautiful. At the same time, I would attempt to imagine how terrified he was, envisioning what his life would be like in this current state. No, I couldn't 100 percent know the depths of his experience. That was impossible. But I could try with all my might to put myself in his place, to feel his loss and his sense of disappearing from a life he had lived for over sixty years. During the days we spent together in the hospital, I would at times get into his bed with him and try to intuit what he was feeling. When the aftereffects of some of his treatments and surgeries deprived him of of his ability to eat food, tell a joke, or take a walk with our grandchildren, and he sometimes fell into a state of despair, I desperately wanted to do what I could to help bring joy back into his life. From these experiences, steeped in empathy, came an incredibly deep-rooted sense of what it was like to be Roger, facing what he was facing. Then something quite remarkable happened: my empathy ran so deep that I began to anticipate his thoughts and needs. We developed an emotional understanding so strong that it became a mental telepathy of sorts. It was one that continued far beyond his time leaving this earth.

I learned so much from going through the journey of cancer with him. Roger is us. He is every one of us. We've all known someone who was sick, dying, or disabled, or who has had some change in life that transformed him or her in possibly unwanted ways. Director Steve James ultimately said about the film, "[It is] a movie about how to live your life with great exuberance and passion and humanity…it's also a movie about how to die." To this day, I am uplifted when I watch *Life Itself* and see the twinkle in Roger's eye. Even on his very last day, he had such a big smile on his face. Sometimes I watch the film and just marvel at his bravery and gumption. He wasn't going to let life defeat him. He could be stubborn and willful, because that was who he was, but that and his belief in encouraging empathy served to keep him going right until the end.

As Roger and I found our way through his final months together, I made him a promise: to do my part to make each day interesting and worth living. Since his death, it has been my fervent desire for the qualities of forgiveness, empathy, compassion, and kindness (what I call the FECK principles) to spread in such a viral way that they become natural parts of the lives of every human being on this planet. Sharing the totality of what FECK represents is the next step in the work Roger and I began together. Most of the principles became clear to me the year before Roger took his "leave of presence," as he called it. One morning, I woke up filled with the clarity of an idea of universal connectedness and was overcome by a commitment to achieve it. My heart was bursting with the knowing that large-scale positive impacts of greater love and unity were achievable if we were willing to come together and spend time putting them into practice. To the principle of empathy that Roger championed, I added forgiveness, compassion, and kindness. Collectively, these four principles not only form the acronym FECK, but they also form the act of "giving a FECK."

Giving a FECK is a unifying journey that begins with forgiveness, the reduction of inner barriers and weight; moves into empathy, the feeling state; then grows into compassion, the willingness to do something; and culminates in kindness, putting all the principles into action.

Forgiveness: The potential impact of giving a FECK is not possible without forgiveness—the ability to see others' perspectives and realize or accept that perhaps they are doing the best they can with what they have available to them. Or, more importantly, the ability to let go of anger or resentment toward another person in order to free yourself from the weight of bitterness and allow yourself to move forward.

Empathy: Once forgiveness has taken place, we can begin to embrace empathy. By putting ourselves in someone else's shoes, we can realize that we are all one and that the survival of our species is not possible without such sensitivity. Empathy is a big part of the picture; it is the necessary precursor to being kinder and more compassionate.

Compassion: From the ability to feel what it is like to be someone else stems the desire to want to do something about it, to help alleviate their suffering. This is what compassion is all about—the heart's desire to take intentional action. Compassion is a personal mission that can start in the heart or the head, but it results in reaching out to support and raise the spirits of another person or people.

Kindness: Bringing everything full circle, kindness is what we do to create forgiveness, to show empathy and compassion at the deepest level, and it is given to help alleviate suffering. It is the actionable uplifting of others in their daily lives, careers, and communities. We can commit acts of kindness every day in ways big or small, and by taking on such acts on a regular basis, we build a kindness muscle that continually gets stronger.

Wherever you are in the world and in your life, what can you offer in the name of forgiveness, empathy, compassion, and kindness? What can you give to your community? To your neighbor? To your colleague or friend?

Contributions in the name of love are what move our world forward, toward a place of greater connection and unity. Giving a FECK is a movement toward achieving greater unity and love for all—a movement that is needed now more than ever. It's about taking these matters to heart and choosing to become a part of the conversation. It is also about sharing the philosophical principles that matter for the betterment of our local and global societies. The four FECK principles are what will help progress our culture along in a more orderly manner and make this a more pleasant world in which to live.

If a virus, such as COVID-19, can replicate and insinuate its structure into the bodies and consciousness of millions of human beings on this planet, affecting us as it has, why, then, can't the same hold true for our ability to spread love and the generative principles of forgiveness, empathy, compassion, and kindness? In the wake of the coronavirus pandemic, we had in many ways begun to act as an impassioned, caring collective as we had never done before. We helped one another navigate lockdowns, celebrated front-line responders, and found a way to rally together to support people in the greatest need. Our hearts opened, making room for greater patience, tolerance, understanding, gratitude, and caring. We had enhanced sympathy with others. The positive strides in human behavior stemming from what we experienced as a collective, global society had the potential to be even more powerful *if sustained.*

If you give a FECK about changing the way things are—and bringing more love for life itself, for yourself, and for others into your day-to-day existence—this book will give you the encouragement, inspiration, examples, and strategies to move you into action and allow you to make the kind of personal contributions, big or small, that will fill your heart and the hearts of others. This guide, with its actionable steps, is for those who aspire to be the emotional leaders or game changers in their circles, communities, or societies. It also presents a powerful antidote to loneliness. This work is about not thinking of people outside our circumstances as "others," because there will always be some people in the world experiencing our circumstances and feeling the same emotions we are feeling. There will also always be someone willing to help and ample opportunities for us to step up and show we care too. There is good that can come from even the most frightening times in our shared history.

It's time to give a FECK.
It doesn't matter who you are
or where you came from—
now is the moment to find
your voice and become a
part of something bigger,
in the name of universal love.

We all have the ability to transform empathy into action for even greater, more positive personal and global impact. Starting today, we can ask ourselves: *Where do we go from here? Are we properly equipped to move forward in such a way that we embrace this brave new world together? What can we do to prove to one another that we really are in this as one? What can we change within our families and communities to create greater unity? What can we do to harness more love on a global scale?*

By choosing to embrace and implement these FECK principles, we experience and promote the best of what this life has to offer, increasing happiness, unity, and joy, and reducing anger, fear, loneliness, and anxiety. We come to understand our impact, value, and role in humanity. We bring about deeper and more meaningful relationships with our partners, families, friends, and peers. We learn ways to work with our neighbors to initiate positive activism in our schools and towns. By doing so, we will be affecting the kind of positive change that helps us realize *we truly are all in this together.*

THE FECK PRINCIPLES

FECK PRINCIPLE 1

Forgiveness

Finding a Way Forward

IN MAY 2008, I stood in the Abraham Lincoln Presidential Library in Springfield, Illinois, ready to take South African archbishop Desmond Tutu to the vault where the private letters of the sixteenth president of the United States, Abraham Lincoln, were stored. As board members from the Lincoln Leadership Prize selection committee, a few of us had gathered for this rare opportunity prior to the official recognition event to follow in Chicago. I had nominated Archbishop Tutu after he and I shared time together in South Africa through Anant Singh, a South African filmmaker who was producing a movie about Nelson Mandela, and the archbishop was to be that year's recipient. The award was established to honor those who had committed to a lifetime of service in the tradition of Abraham Lincoln, evidencing "great strength of character, individual conscience and an unwavering commitment to the defining principles of democracy."[1] The board agreed unanimously that the principles of the award were steadfast within Archbishop Tutu.

As we discussed matters of race and politics, I was struck by the archbishop's easygoing manner and his capacity to break out into a big smile or a hearty laugh. Even after everything that had happened to his country under the old apartheid regime, he seemed to have made peace with himself and others.

As Archbishop Tutu and I prepared to handle Lincoln's original letters, we each donned a pair of white gloves. I stood listening raptly, watching the emotions dance across his face as he read each of them. One of the letters had been written by Lincoln during his deliberations over the 1863 Emancipation Proclamation. Within it was declared "'that all persons held as slaves' within the rebellious states 'are, and henceforward shall be free.'"[2] Tutu read the words silently at first, then aloud. He flipped through both sides of the document, over and over again, as if processing its every word. After a deep sigh, he shared that the weight of Lincoln's words paralleled some of the deep issues that he and Nelson Mandela had to consider during the administration of the Truth and Reconciliation Commission. In July 1995, South Africa's new parliament had passed a law authorizing the formation of the commission, an organization whose objective was to "promote reconciliation and forgiveness among perpetrators and victims of apartheid." President Nelson Mandela appointed Archbishop Tutu to chair it. The commission took the testimony of nearly twenty-one thousand victims.[3] Archbishop Tutu said that he lost many friends over the concepts of their commission, but he and President Mandela knew there would be no peace and no progress without forgiveness. Furthermore, there would be no forgiveness without specific admissions of guilt or atrocities committed under apartheid. In exchange for those truths and admissions of guilt, the South African government, through the Truth and Reconciliation Commission, had to provide a path for redemption.

After Nelson Mandela was arrested in 1962, he was sentenced to life imprisonment for conspiring to overthrow the state. Facing a possible death sentence, he told the courts, "During my lifetime I have dedicated myself to this struggle of the African people. I have fought against white domination, and I have fought against Black domination. I have cherished the ideal of a democratic and free society in which all persons live together in harmony with equal opportunities. It is an ideal which I hope to live for and to achieve. But if needs be, it is an ideal for which I am prepared to die."[4]

During that visit to South Africa, I was privileged to spend time with Ahmed Kathrada (nickname "Kathy"), who had also been sentenced to life imprisonment with Mandela and other African National Congress members for their anti-apartheid activism. He had taken me on a tour of his cell at Robben Island and of Nelson Mandela's cell. It was a profoundly surreal experience. As I stood in that little cell, my mind could not reconcile how the kind man standing before me could be almost casual about what had happened to him and Nelson Mandela. It was almost as if, in listening to him, it had all happened to someone else. Just when I felt as though I couldn't be much more awestruck, he then introduced me to the prison's "tour guide" and explained this man had been one of their jailers during their period of imprisonment. They were now friends. How could that be? When Kathy and I were able to find some time alone,

I asked him how this had all been possible. He told me he had forgiven the jailer. In fact, he was grateful for that man, as he had been the one to make sure he, Mandela, and others were given food and had treated them like human beings, rather than criminals. Kathy confirmed to me the role forgiveness played in his life. He said that without it, mentally he would still be in that prison cell.

After he was released from Victor Verster Prison in February 1990, Mandela did not seek revenge on those who had been responsible for his captivity. Instead, he sought reconciliation and continued his unwavering commitment to transforming South Africa into a democratic and free society in which all persons live together in harmony with equal opportunities. The world watched as he transformed from prisoner to the president of South Africa. It was the most amazing thing to me.

Forgiveness has the power to free us and allow us to move forward in peace.

As I stood next to the man who chaired the commission alongside President Mandela, I remained in awe and wonder at how the two of them had been able to do so without rancor after what had happened to them under the unjust system of racial apartheid. When the opportunity arrived, I asked Archbishop Tutu the one question that had continued to puzzle me the most: How could Nelson Mandela not feel bitterness or want revenge after being imprisoned for twenty-seven years because of his beliefs in equality? Mandela's strength and accomplishments had always left a profoundly deep impression on me. I wondered how he could have gone from being denied basic freedoms for decades to rallying far-reaching support for the peaceful movement to end the legacy of apartheid. Where was his anger? Where was his call for revenge or justice? Who was this man who could put aside his personal sacrifices for the good of his country and humankind? And how was he able to do so without the bloodshed others may have called for?

Tutu sighed as he continued to read Lincoln's letters while pondering my question. He then answered, "Without forgiveness there is nothing. You remain a prisoner. Without forgiveness the nation cannot move forward." To him, forgiveness was not only a biblical prerequisite but one of political expediency. "Without forgiveness," he repeated, "we remain locked in our pain and cannot achieve freedom or reconciliation."

Many authors and twelve-step recovery programs describe resentment as a poison you drink hoping it will kill someone else.[5] It always made me laugh when I heard people say that, but it's true. Resentment and failure to forgive really do poison us. They distort our insight and skew the way we look at the world. While some creative types may be able to channel their anger or resentment into producing great works of art, for most of us, any kind of resentment dampens our creativity and reduces our ability to be happy. Channeled or not, when we continue to carry resentment, consciously or subconsciously, it weighs heavily on our spirits, until it is released through forgiveness.

Forgiveness can be powerful even in small doses or through the simplest actions.

Our full capacity to contribute in the name of love starts with a foundation of forgiveness. When someone or something has hurt us, forgiveness must come first if we have any chance of fully opening ourselves up to empathy, compassion, and kindness. That is the beginning of giving a FECK. Forgiveness is the ability to let go of anger or resentment toward someone else so as to free ourselves from the weight of bitterness and allow ourselves to move forward. *Handbook of Forgiveness* defines the forgiveness of others as "a response that holds an offender responsible for an offense while replacing negative thoughts, emotions, and behaviors toward the offender with prosocial responses."[6] Forgiveness researcher Fred Luskin, PhD, director of the Stanford University Forgiveness Projects and the author of the best-selling book *Forgive for Good: A Proven Prescription for Health and Happiness* and coauthor of *Stress Free for Good: 10 Scientifically Proven Life Skills for Health and Happiness*, calls forgiveness "an assertive creation of peace in the present" and says that "forgiveness is the experience of being at peace right now."[7]

Big or small, every effort in the name of forgiveness has an impact. We all get to choose how we feel in this moment, and how any required forgiveness directs our level or lack of peace. Forgiveness is not intended to be an overwhelming endeavor, nor should it take a lot of effort for it to make a big difference. We do not all have to reach the heights of forgiveness achieved by South African President Nelson Mandela, though if finding peace or moving through to empathy, compassion, and kindness is our goal, we must begin with forgiveness.

Lifting the Burden

ON JUNE 17, 2015, in Charleston, South Carolina, self-proclaimed white supremacist Dylann Roof entered the prayer service at the historic Emanuel African Methodist Episcopal Church and opened fire, killing nine members of the congregation. The event marked one of the deadliest attacks ever in an American place of worship. Roof was arrested the next morning and later sentenced to life in prison, without parole. Two days after the shootings, survivors Felicia Sanders, Polly Sheppard, and Jennifer Pinckney said that they forgave Roof. Sanders lost her aunt and twenty-six-year-old son in the attack; Pinckney lost her husband, Pastor Clementa Pinckney. President Barack Obama gave the eulogy at Clementa's funeral.

I was humbled and reduced to tears as I considered how these women were able to summon that almost divine resolve to forgive after suffering the loss of their loved ones. Even today, I tear up when I think about it. Where does that profound capacity come from? In an interview on *TODAY*, the three women shared their message about the power and purpose of forgiveness. After being inspired by Felicia Sanders's ability to forgive so quickly, Polly Sheppard knew that she needed to forgive alongside her friend. Reflecting on how she approached forgiveness, she said, "You think that you are letting someone else off the hook, but you are actually letting yourself off the hook, because if you keep [the hatred], there is no healing. You have to love each other."[8]

Resentment and anger take up space in our heads and in our hearts, taking away space from light, love, and good positive feelings.

LIFTING THE BURDEN

Have you ever wondered why we use the phrase *It feels like a weight has been lifted from my shoulders*? When we've been wounded or have thoughts of revenge, the resulting emotions are often accompanied by a sense of inferiority, helplessness, and victimization. Asking to be relieved of these feelings frees us of that mental and emotional weight. By lifting the burden, forgiveness creates openness and light. There is one powerful point about all of this that we so easily forget: Often, the person against whom we have resentment may not even know we harbor those feelings. We can be carrying all that weight on our shoulders while that person is walking around, living life, not thinking about us at all!

I am all too human. On occasion, I have wanted to be vengeful more than I have wanted to be compassionate. I mistakenly believed that my power was in getting back at someone rather than in trying to resolve the issue. In actuality, that was not a source of power. The first time I clearly remember intently praying and meditating about a situation in which I felt unfairly slighted, I had no expectations. Faced with a hurt I had been carrying around for far too long, I was finally ready to surrender. I wanted to move forward. And I was looking for a way to start framing the situation differently.

After meditating about it, I got on my knees that night, just before going to bed, and asked to be shown the path to forgiveness. When I woke up the next morning, I could not believe how much lighter and sunnier everything seemed! It became clear to me that I had been carrying the burden of anger for far too long. Miraculously, after this intense session of prayer and meditation, the thirst for revenge had been lifted. When I thought of my adversaries, there were no longer strong hateful thoughts attached to them. I was able to think about the situation dispassionately for the first time. No longer was I imprisoned. Concentrating on getting back at someone had kept me in a victim mentality. I was freed only after taking affirmative steps in the process of forgiving. The truth was that it never felt right wanting revenge, which is why the concept of forgiveness is so big. It helps keep humanity in the lead and liberates us from the bonds of hatred, anger, resentment, and so many other emotions that rob us of our ability to live with happiness.

The psychological benefits of forgiveness have

been studied. As part of their 2023 study, researchers Suzanne Freedman and Eva Yi-Ju Chen initiated a ten-week forgiveness education program for two classes of fifth graders attending a low-income school in a midwestern city of the United States. The participating students showed significantly increased forgiveness toward the specific person who had hurt them and greater knowledge and understanding about forgiveness in general at the end of the program. Their responses also indicated that they had developed a greater willingness to forgive in other situations of hurt and conflict.[9]

A 2019 study published in the *Journal of Psychological Thought* suggests that children's forgiveness plays a significant role in their social, emotional, and interpersonal development. Earlier studies, focused primarily on forgiveness among adults, suggest that forgiveness is "closely linked with a host of positive life outcomes for people across all developmental periods" and that it tends to provide an enhanced quality of relationships, general happiness, satisfaction, and well-being. While the children's study found that kids "easily accepted their wrongdoings" and their forgiveness of others was observed to be "explicit," this was especially true when significant others (e.g., parents, teachers, and caregivers) had a facilitative role.[10] This is to say that the more we can teach ourselves and our children to forgive, the more emotionally empowered we will likely all grow to be.

Freeing ourselves of angst and anger toward another person allows us to begin to let the light in.

To this day, when there is a need for forgiveness, I pray and meditate. My prayers are usually nonpartisan. I pray for my family and friends, and for their health and happiness. I pray for wisdom for our leaders and for the well-being of all the people on this earth. I pray for the care of the climate and the universe. I pray for health, clarity, and an open heart for myself. For those who are not tolerant of other people, I pray that their hearts will open. I pray to be surrounded by love and light and to be able to spread them to others. I pray to increase my own tolerance and patience. I pray for mercy. And I pray for forgiveness—both to forgive and to be forgiven. When I want to be able to forgive a particular person, I pray and ask to be relieved of any revenge, hate, disbelief, or intolerance I may be feeling. I ask to be shown a clear direction and a way past the resentment or hurt I am holding. Any one of us can pray for someone else's evolution along with our own. It isn't as much about how we pray or meditate, or to whom we are praying; what matters is that we undertake the process of forgiveness.

When it comes to how we can best forgive in more general situations, Fred Luskin recommends the following:

- Become more grateful: Open your heart to what you have. Focus on the fact that the world did give you enough.
- Manage the stress of the unforgiveness: Without proper work to calm our nervous systems, stress can take over and cause our thinking to become narrow and hostile.

- Change the story you tell: Avoid becoming attached to any story that paints you as a helpless victim. A story of helplessness can even be worse than the events that have happened to us.
- Prove that there was an error and you did not deserve what you received.[11]

Carrying thoughts of hatred, intolerance, violence, or revenge toward someone also clouds our minds so much that we cannot think clearly about how to handle a situation or how to approach that person to engage in meaningful dialogue. Holding in anger is like putting a shield up against that person or situation. We may think we've blocked the anger, but whether we feel it consciously or not, the emotion can still weigh heavily on us and prevent us from moving forward. The amazing thing about intently concentrating on or asking for forgiveness is that we will know when it is working. Even through a simple meditation, we can bring forth the person or situation we need to forgive and ask for clarity and to heal that person or situation. This is necessary for all of us, because in order to increase the space in our hearts for loving ourselves or reaching out to other people, we must clear out the space that hurt and anger occupy. And one of the ways to do that is to find it within ourselves to forgive.

Not an Easy Process

IT WAS ALMOST IMPOSSIBLE to comprehend what the Amish community of Nickel Mines in Lancaster County, Pennsylvania, chose to do amid one of the greatest tragedies in its history. On October 2, 2006, thirty-two-year-old milk-truck driver Charles Roberts burst into a one-room schoolhouse armed with an arsenal of weapons. He ordered the boys in the class to help him tow in supplies that included lumber, wires, chains, nails, tools, and ammunition. After lining up the children in the front of the room, he let the fifteen boys and two adults leave. Then he proceeded to barricade the doors with two-by-fours and tie up the girls who remained inside.[12] He began firing in rapid succession, killing five of the girls at close range and wounding several others before taking his own life as police arrived.[13] Witnesses say that when state troopers arrived, Roberts panicked. He called his wife to tell her that he wasn't coming home. It is uncertain what Roberts intended to do that day. A list of his materials and four suicide notes, written respectively to his wife and children, were later found by the authorities. Those notes described him as being "mad at God" for the loss of his daughter, Elise, who had been prematurely born, and in a note he left for his wife, Roberts revealed that he had molested two young relatives twenty years earlier and was having fantasies about committing such acts again.

On that very same day, members of the Nickel Mines Amish community took food to the gunman's widow, Marie Roberts. They spoke with her about forgiveness. There is an Amish proverb that states, "Instead of putting others in their place, put yourself in their place." Six days after the shootings, the same families who had just buried their daughters attended Charles Roberts's funeral. It was also reported that funds donated from around the world were given by the Amish community to the killer's family, even though the surviving victims faced significant medical bills. The community's selfless actions fostered forgiveness and reconciliation. Marie Roberts later released a written statement thanking the Amish community and other local people for their "forgiveness, grace and mercy."[14]

It doesn't matter whether the person intended to harm us when they did so; that's not a burden we should carry forward.

For the longest time, I could not wrap my head around how the community, family members, and especially the parents of those innocent young girls could bring themselves to do what they did. It was something that stuck with me for years. Even today, when I think of or talk about it, my throat catches with emotion. How could such a degree of forgiveness exist? First, I believe it is because the community came together to forgive. As a 2018 study published in the *Journal of Positive Psychology* concludes, "Community-based approaches are a viable method of promoting forgiveness that may serve as a less intense but more easily disseminated and less costly approach to promoting forgiveness than traditional modalities of psychological treatment."[15]

When we are faced with the need to forgive, it can be greatly beneficial to join forces with our community or a trusted ally to take the next step or talk through our circumstances.

While the people of Nickel Mines had one another's support in reaching the levels of forgiveness they were able to achieve, doing so took time. It wasn't easy, and, as was later learned, it was an ongoing, multilayered effort. Members of the community said their decision to forgive Charles Roberts and his family was not as simple as it appeared. "It's not a once and done thing," said Linda Fisher. "It is a lifelong process." Aaron Esh Jr. was the oldest student present in the schoolhouse the day of the shootings. He conveyed that it was a struggle to stay constant in forgiveness. "You have to fight the bitter thoughts," he said.[16]

Sometimes we are going to have to work a little harder at releasing the resentment. When we are faced with the need to forgive, it can help to talk through the circumstances with someone we trust—a friend, colleague, mentor, therapist, religious leader, or a trusted support group. Discussing our feelings can allow us to start thinking about and opening ourselves to forgiveness. Some of life's greatest challenges will not pass quickly, and the release of anger and resentment will take time. There may also be occasions when we have to "check ourselves." For instance, in one situation where I thought that I had forgiven someone and released all my resentment, I tested my resolve by imagining how I might act if I saw that person again. You can do the same by observing your reactions in situations where you are working to forgive someone. This will help you to know where work remains to be done.

Just as with the Amish community of Nickel Mines, who showed us how they found it within themselves to reach out to all who were affected that day, including the wife of the perpetrator, the power of forgiveness in healing, connection, and unity is truly miraculous. It can help us find light in even the darkest moments—results that are evident when we feel them in our hearts and watch the ripple effects of forgiveness in action.

Before dawn on October 12, ten days after the shootings, the Nickel Mines schoolhouse was demolished. It was one of 150 parent-led, one-room schoolhouses that supported the Amish population of two hundred thousand in a community where there was very little police presence or concern for security because the incidence of crime was so low. A spokesperson coordinating activities with the Amish community told CBS that destroying the school was about trying to reach some closure after the shocking incident.[17] A new one-room schoolhouse called the New Hope Amish School was later built in another location.[18]

The Justice of Forgiveness

IN CREATING HIS DEBUT documentary, *They Call Us Monsters*, director Ben Lear, alongside his editor, Eli Despres, and producers Sasha Alpert and Scott Budnick (*The Hangover*), endeavored to portray the plight of incarcerated youth who had received de facto life sentences for crimes they committed before they were eighteen years old. "*They Call Us Monsters* set out to ask some simple questions: Do young people have a greater capacity for change? Should they be treated differently from adults? Witnessing the incredible transformations the boys have made in the ten years since filming, I think we have our answer," Ben Lear concluded in a conversation we recently had.

The filmmakers compiled footage of court hearings, testimonials from the boys' respective families, and a key interview with a victim. During the film,

Lear enters the juvenile hall in the Los Angeles neighborhood of Sylmar to meet with one of the incarcerated boys. At age twelve, Jarad had witnessed his stepfather attempt suicide by stabbing himself in the chest. The stepfather was certain that his actions caused irreparable damage to his son and couldn't help but burst into tears in court as Jarad faced serious jail time. When the ruling of life in prison was handed down, Jarad simply smirked in disbelief. But after years of working to change and atone, Jarad emerged from prison a seemingly different person. He now works for the California State Capitol and studies criminal justice.

Following a review of his case after he'd served nine years in prison, Jarad's sentence was commuted by the governor of California. He finally had opportunity ahead of him, thanks to the forgiveness of the legal system and his own self-forgiveness. Jarad was an armed passenger in a car during a drive-by shooting that resulted in the paralysis of a young woman. Although it was initially unclear whose bullet struck the woman, over time Jarad was able to admit his culpability, express remorse, apologize, and ask for forgiveness. During his period of incarceration, he also took many steps toward rehabilitating his life and improving his relationships, even when he thought he would be in prison for life. His goal was to be a better person in any interaction.[19]

After viewing the documentary about his time in prison, he told PBS, "It was uncomfortable at first watching myself. I don't know if it's because I was acting like a fool. Nevertheless, it proved to be very insightful because I [saw] how I was coping with pain, hurt and the fact I forfeited my freedom."[20] Jarad said that since the movie was filmed, he has been "striving day after day to become a better person and hopefully re-enter society and just be a citizen, an asset, not a liability." He has made the choice to leave "the criminal lifestyle" in his past. At the time of that interview, he was two semesters away from obtaining an associate degree in business and technology. In his words, "God has me living in the now looking forward and learning from the past. Change is possible but forgiveness is needed."[21]

Sometimes, film portrayals of real-world problems can help us think more empathetically about the need for forgiveness, love, and support. When we're hurting or holding resentment or shame, it's harder to access our higher self or, as Jarad said, to be a better person. Sometimes, by simply sitting down in a place of comfort, quiet, safety, and meditation, we can get in touch with the soul or spirit of who we are. We can communicate with our higher self and ask, *If my higher self were doing this, how would I handle it?*

When it comes to deciding how to proceed in the name of forgiveness, always follow the direction of your higher self.

Martha Minow, former Harvard Law School dean and author of *When Should Law Forgive?*, gave an enlightening 2019 TEDx Talk entitled "How Forgiveness Can Create a More Just Legal System." During her talk, in which she noted that the law leans so severely toward punishment these days, she shared her concerns that lawyers and officials often overlook the tools the law provides to allow for forgiveness. She did, however, single out her former student Barack Obama for his effective application of one of these tools. As president, he used his pardon power to release people from prison after the law changed to provide shorter sentences for the same drug crimes these individuals had been convicted of earlier.

While Minow advocates for the use of such forgiveness tools in criminal matters, she is also clear about the challenges they pose, particularly when they are used with bias. She warns that "forgiveness could undermine the commitment that law has to treat people the same under the same circumstances." As Minow says, "In this age of resentment, mass incarceration, widespread consumer debt, we need more forgiveness, but we need a philosophy of forgiveness."[22] Her words ring true now more than ever, as so many African American men are serving time for drug offenses that are no longer considered criminal acts under new and evolving laws.[23] How do we begin to repair the damage done to families that were decimated by these acts of punishment? Are there some legal means by which forgiveness can wipe the slate clean for them and allow for the start of a rehabilitated new life?

The argument for forgiveness in the law does not advocate being soft on crime.

Minow is clear that we must preserve the rule of law while simultaneously amplifying the law's support for forgiveness. In her words, "We need to forgive fairly.... To ask how law may forgive is not to deny the fact of wrongdoing. Rather, it's to widen the lens to enable glimpses of the larger patterns and enable new choices that can go forward if we can wipe the slate clean."[24] For those heading the criminal justice system, this means applying the law equally and fairly. Minow's exhortation would widen the lens through which we look at instances such as those shared in *They Call Us Monsters* to make sure that we apply the law fairly and take into account both the punishment for the wrong done by the incarcerated youth as well as the fate of their victims, while providing a path for forgiveness and rehabilitation in those instances where they are merited.

Reclaiming Our Personal Power

I GREW UP in a house where compassion and kindness were modeled for me by my parents. Those values became a part of my lifeblood. I grew up with four brothers and four sisters, and humor was a way of life, though we also knew what was important. Education was highly valued and seen as a way to get ahead in the world. But because I was one of nine children, the economics of attaining a higher education was problematic. Throughout my childhood, I did everything in my power to make sure that a postsecondary education was possible for me. In grade school, I was a class officer, the teacher's pet, and the class salutatorian . . . though I was admittedly also sometimes the class clown. Our home was always filled with books, and my sister Adele, a voracious reader, was my idol. I followed her lead.

When I was in high school and out sick with the mumps, both my algebra and my computer science teachers called my home to ask how I was doing. During that call, I overheard my father telling them what a good girl I was, smart and studious. He said I was always reading or helping out around the house. I had no idea he paid such close attention to what I did with so many siblings coming and going. While I was a bit surprised that my teachers cared enough to call, I was even more surprised to hear my father say how proud he was of me. My father was of that generation of men who showed their love by quietly providing for their families, but who didn't really give a lot of compliments. My mother's pride was easier to see. I would notice it when she accompanied me to luncheons hosted for top students by the National Honor Society. We would wear our hats and white gloves; she would make sure I knew which fork or utensil to use for each dish. And she sparkled in conversation with the other students and parents. She never doubted that I wouldn't continue my education, and she was determined to assist in any way she could. She was also lavish in her praises and in communicating that she loved us dearly.

When I was sixteen years old, I graduated from high school. My parents were elated and had so much hope for my future. My sister Adele had attended a junior college, and my sisters Martha and Carrie had gone to vocational schools to become nursing assistants. I would be the first of their nine children to attend a four-year college. Then it happened. During my first year living away from home and attending college, I discovered I was pregnant. I feared telling my family. No one in our family had had a baby out of wedlock. I didn't want to be the first one to cause such shame for them. Even though the hippies were bringing in an era of free love in the late 1960s and early 1970s, society was still using terms such as "out of wedlock" and shaming unwed mothers, especially if they were Black, for having what were condescendingly called "illegitimate" children. In 1969, abortions were illegal. Some of my university colleagues from wealthier families told me I could obtain what was referred to in the newspapers as a "back-alley abortion," but it would would cost money I didn't have. I also had no idea how to find or navigate that underworld. (It is unfathomable to me that over fifty years later, the issue of a woman's right to choose is once again headline news.)

A few months into my pregnancy, I landed in the hospital after taking some unrelated pills. The attending physician told me, "Young lady, you're pregnant and you're not going to leave this hospital until you tell your family." Admitting to my parents that I was pregnant was one of the hardest things I've ever had to do. As the doctor handed me the phone to call them, I was trembling, scared, and ashamed. I felt as though I had betrayed my family's trust in me. For so long, I had lived up to their expectations, having been the "good girl," the "smart girl," the "caring one," and the "leader." Now all I could think was, *How could this happen to me? How could I let my family down?* When I spoke with them, I was tearful and apologetic. To my surprise, they didn't excoriate me or make me feel more shame. Instead, as the tears streamed down my face, my parents told me they loved me and immediately began to work out a plan for how I would continue school. They all were so loving and so kind. My mother said, "Just bring the baby home." The only question from my oldest brother, Johnnie, and my sister-in-law Eunice was,

"How are you?" In that moment, I realized that the only person from whom I needed forgiveness was myself.

Sometimes we just need to know that someone cares, so that we can begin the process of forgiveness.

My family's love, acceptance, and belief in me gave me the start I needed to eventually forgive myself. I had to let myself truly feel their support and realize that I was worthy of it all. As I am writing this, tears are streaming down my face once again. This memory and part of my life is one I don't allow to take up space in my head too often, though today I am letting the tears flow. They are not tears of self-pity but rather tears of gratitude for the wonderful people who surrounded me with such unconditional love. Without the crucial support of my family and closest college classmates, I probably would have been overwhelmed by feelings of shame and may have dropped out of school. When it came time to ask my children for permission to include this personal story, they gave it unreservedly.

Forgiveness is about choosing the more positive and affirmative ways to reach the point of reclaiming our personal power. It's about asking what else we can do to make the situation not seem as weighty or not make us feel as if we're a victim of our circumstances. *Handbook of Forgiveness* references one of the earliest definitions of self-forgiveness, offered by R. D. Enright and the Human Development Study Group (1996): "A willingness to abandon self-resentment in the face of one's own acknowledged objective wrong, while fostering compassion, generosity, and love toward oneself."[25] What's more is the significant association between the higher levels of self-forgiveness (or self-compassion!) and lower levels of self-harm or suicidal ideation.[26] It is my hope that this will lead us all to want to offer ourselves greater self-forgiveness.

Self-forgiveness is never something we should feel ashamed to embrace. Rather, it should be appreciated as something that frees us from humiliation, guilt, and self-criticism. What's important to remember is that, for any of us, self-forgiveness must be learned and practiced in order for us to be able to open ourselves up to others' perspectives—to forgive, have empathy for, and be compassionate with them. Forgiveness and self-forgiveness are the starting points to living more fully, more peacefully, and more joyfully. Self-forgiveness empowered me to pick up the pieces and keep going through the great challenge of finishing my degree as a young mother. I wed my first husband, Merle, moved to the married students' residence off campus, had a second child, finished college, entered and completed graduate school, went on to earn my juris doctor degree, and became a lawyer. Being a mother has been one of the most gratifying things I have ever done. Self-forgiveness gave me the foundational tools to shift my perception about my situation and moved me forward to make a better life for my children.

Forgiving ourselves happens once we allow ourselves to accept all the goodness, kindness, and love other people are giving us.

People often look disapprovingly on young mothers. Sometimes, though, having a child so early in life can be a blessing. Much depends on how you handle it and how much support you have. Make no mistake about it, that is a decision that should be made between a woman, her doctor, and her family. In my case, having two children to care for so early in life opened up my heart. I became a mother lioness. I knew I wanted to create a better world for my son, my daughter, and, later, my grandchildren. I also wanted the way I moved through the world to be an example for them. Learning to forgive myself allowed me to teach them and others about the power of forgiveness. Being unconditionally accepted by other people and extending compassion to myself helps me even today in administering programs that award grants and scholarships and mentorship opportunities to young people. I know how important it was to have someone listen to me and encourage me in my educational and career pursuits. I am still paying it forward to this day.

Finding Common Ground

IN NOVEMBER 2020, when Joe Biden was declared the winner of the US presidential election, Kamala Harris became not only the first woman but also the first Black and first Asian American vice president. Where I live in Chicago, people were honking their car horns, dancing in the streets, and forming groups on the corners to proclaim joy in the election results. These images were broadcast on television and cable news stations and posted across the internet. It was the popular saying "If you can see it, you can be it" playing out in real life. For the first time in the history of our nation, little girls and boys were seeing a woman as vice president, and little Black and brown girls were seeing a woman who looked like them. In the almost 250-year history of the United States, this was groundbreaking.

But this momentous occasion seemed only to exacerbate the divide within our nation. At a time when we should have been celebrating, the happiness was short lived. President Trump immediately challenged the election as fraudulent (even after the valid state and federal officials, some appointed by Trump, found no evidence of fraud and dismissed more than fifty lawsuits filed by Trump and his allies).[27] The reactions to the election by certain factions crippled communities and divided family connections already rattled by the effects of the coronavirus pandemic. Then came the surreal violence and riots that ensued at the US Capitol on January 6, 2021, as the doors and windows of the building that represents the very center of American democracy were breached. Millions were left shocked and lives were lost after the terrifying insurrection. Given our history of peaceful transfer of power for more than two centuries, an event like this in present-day America was unthinkable before the attack.

Daily news reports echoed the mounting cries for justice. Alongside these events, the protests that began after the death of George Floyd, a Black man who was killed in Minneapolis by police in May

2020, continued. Floyd's death was ruled a homicide, leading to a global call to action in the name of racial reconciliation and social justice for all. Polarization over these issues not only persisted but escalated. Pleas for national unity to preserve our democracy reached a deafening pitch, as many looked into the abyss and were shaken by the thought of what could be. In the end, we were collectively facing an intense need to bring our nation and our world back together. A suppressed energy, held for so long, had bubbled over into a need to take action and initiate something concrete to resonate on a large scale. People challenging the status quo wanted to see the kind of lasting impact that would fuel a sustained shift in our global society.

In difficult times such as these, it can help to look beyond our own turmoil for answers, which brings me to a very important movie I viewed in 2016. Filmmakers Stephen Apkon and Andrew Young, as well as story consultant Marcina Hale, were invited guests at the Ebertfest film festival at the University of Illinois at Urbana-Champaign that year. There we previewed their documentary, *Disturbing the Peace*. The film presented a unique perspective on the Israeli-Palestinian conflict and posed the question: What would happen if both sides of the conflict made a conscious decision to lay down their weapons and work toward forgiveness and peace? Watching the film felt like being struck by a lightning bolt, providing a visceral opening into a point of new possibility in the face of conventional wisdom, which often dictates that the conflicts between the Israelis and the Palestinians are too old, deep seated, and complex for a solution.

In an interview with the film's codirector Stephen Apkon (who is also the founder of the Jacob Burns Film Center in Pleasantville, New York), he shared with me that the documentary was much more than the one he set out to make. He was researching a potential film project in the region but felt that there was nothing new to say about the decades-long conflict between Israel and Palestine. By coincidence, he then met the group of men and women who called themselves "Combatants for Peace" and saw something completely original. They were former enemy combatants who had taken part in the violence on opposite sides and ultimately laid down their weapons, came together, and chose to work through nonviolence to end the conflict. In their words, they were a "community of people taking responsibility for their own creation."[28]

Choosing forgiveness means that we choose to create deeper relationships and greater human decency.

By 2021, I wished that we could superimpose the power of forgiveness displayed by the Israelis and Palestinians featured in this movie onto the many sectors of our nation that still remained at odds. *Disturbing the Peace* had so clearly showcased how even people fighting against one another because of complex historical events—people echoing a mutual hatred that had run so deep for so long that they believed it could never be reconciled—had finally decided to bond together to find common ground. They had done so against extraordinary odds and with the force of mutual forgiveness. When I saw that documentary for the first time, it filled me with such hope for all humanity. It felt more like a movement than a movie, inspiring me to see more clearly the connection between forgiveness, empathy, and compassion. Causing me, in fact, to add forgiveness as step one of the four-step FECK formula. It also became the first film to be awarded the Ebert Humanitarian Award.

On October 7, 2023, the group Hamas staged a brutal surprise attack killing and kidnapping of Israelis. I have thought about the movie *Disturbing the Peace* every day since that attack and am writing this as the world pivots to figure out how to address the atrocities without exacerbating a humanitarian crisis for Palestinians. When I contacted Apkon, the film's codirector, to ask whether the Combatants for Peace could supply any hope of intervening in the process, he wrote a very nuanced and complex article about his views of the situation. In our discussion about the article, he concluded that after all the military and political actions have been taken, he hopes that the two words he saw painted on the walls during one of his visits to Israel will prevail: "Love Wins."

Empathy, compassion, and kindness, and their subsequent impact, are not possible without forgiveness.

If President Lincoln could identify and implement solutions to take on the monumental tasks of ending slavery and saving a nation divided, and if Nelson Mandela and Archbishop Desmond Tutu could dedicate their lives to ending the system of apartheid and transitioning South Africa to a country of equal protection under the law, without bloodshed, then we, as humanity, can surely find a way to work through and heal the divisions that have developed in our country and the world during recent times. That is my fervent hope.

Forgiveness Journal

Sometimes we have to confront a particularly difficult challenge in our business, personal, or community settings before the path to forgiveness can open up. The following pages offer exercises and questions to help unblock and strengthen your forgiveness muscles. When it comes to forgiving, there are times when we simply have to sit down and write things out in order to release them.

Forgiveness Exercise 1: The Pros and Cons

I'm a big supporter of writing out both pros and cons. Consider the following questions as you make a list of the pros and cons of a situation where forgiveness is required.

What is it about this situation that I think is unfair?

How is it making me feel?

How would I feel if I was able to forgive or see this situation from another perspective?

Choosing to Forgive

Pros	Cons

Forgiveness Exercise 2: The Encounter

To test yourself before possibly encountering the person or people you are trying to forgive, ask yourself the following questions.

How does it feel to picture myself face-to-face with that person? ______________________

____

____

____

____

What emotions are likely to surface if I visit that person's social media profile? ______________________

____

____

____

____

____

____

Would I try to avoid them if I saw them on the street?

____

____

____

____

Would I keep my distance if I was in a room with them at an event? Have I forgiven the person or people (and myself!) enough to walk up to them, say hello, and be civil?

___

___

___

___

___

___

___

___

___

___

___

___

Being able to do any of these things doesn't mean we have to become fast friends with the person we have forgiven . . . but the exercise helps us check in with ourselves to see the progress we have made! If we are able to see that person or those people and not feel anger, we can show gratitude and love toward ourselves for coming that far and being able to do so. From there we can continue to work on building greater forgiveness over time.

Forgiveness Exercise 3: Self-Forgiveness

Only once we have embraced and acted in forgiveness can we open ourselves to all that is waiting to come our way through empathy, compassion, and kindness. Use this exercise to dive into areas of your life where you need to forgive yourself.

In the space following each prompt, write how you feel and what you will do to forgive yourself. Be sure to talk about your situation or feelings in the way you want them to be, rather than how they currently are. Use *present-tense statements* instead of writing about something in future tense.

And remember as you are responding, ask yourself how your higher self might reply.

If I could move forward without this weight of anger, I would feel . . . ________________________

____

____

____

____

____

____

____

____

If I wasn't so resentful, I would be able to . . .

___

___

___

___

___

Without the weight of anger toward myself or someone else, I would be . . . ___

___

___

___

___

___

Then repeat your statements to yourself, always in the present tense, and end the exercise by saying, *I am free. I am liberated. I am happy.*

You can also send what you've written to yourself. Seal your answers in an envelope and give them to someone you trust to mail them to you in a month. Seeing what you wrote in your own handwriting weeks later can look and feel very different. Also, comparing where you were a month or two earlier to where you are (or have grown to) now can help put everything in perspective. When you receive your answers in the mail, use them to check in with yourself and see how far you have progressed in your forgiveness of yourself and/or others. Sometimes, letters deepen our conversation with ourselves and can truly help us to evolve.

FECK PRINCIPLE 2

Empathy

We're All in This Together

EVER SINCE the first motion picture was released, we, as a society, have been entranced with the film industry. For some filmmakers and viewers, movies can provide an entertaining break from our sometimes-stressful realities. While I understand and appreciate the motivation behind these types of films, I usually lean toward movies with good storytelling that humanize our experiences. Neuroscience studies even support that when we see a movie with car chases, explosions, and people being unkind to or killing one another, we are more likely to experience road rage on our way home from the theater.[29] Personally I have noticed that I am apt to drive faster, listen to music with the volume turned up, and talk louder in the moments following such films. When we watch a movie where people are being kind to one another and doing good things, the hope is that the movie leads to us going out into the world and being more thoughtful toward others. I am not saying there is a direct causation or a one-to-one correlation between what a film portrays and how we act after watching it, but making and watching movies that unify humanity can have an undeniable impact . . . and who wouldn't want more good in the world?

Roger's message, right up to his last breath on April 4, 2013, was one of empathy. He liked to define empathy as "knowing what it's like to be a person of a different race, gender, age, political background, religion, or socioeconomic circumstance, and respecting those differences." He adamantly proclaimed that film is one of the best media in which to convey empathy. Great movies, he said, let you "live somebody else's life, a little bit, for a while," allowing us, one film at a time, to step into other people's shoes, to experience vicariously what it feels like to be them. Movies allow us to understand more about what it's like to live in a different country, be of a different ethnicity, work in a different profession, experience joblessness, or have different hopes, dreams, aspirations, and fears.

Roger felt fortunate that his chosen profession as a film critic was a gateway to gaining insight into people. He had an unshakable belief that great movies enlarge and civilize us.

Empathy is critical to our showcasing care for the human condition.

So how else is empathy defined? Stanford psychologist Jamil Zaki and Harvard psychologist Mina Cikara tell us in their 2015 article, "Addressing Empathic Failures," that empathy is "people's sharing and understanding of each other's emotions." They state that it "bolsters relationships, improves individuals' well-being, and promotes prosocial behavior."[30] *The Routledge Handbook of Philosophy of Empathy* defines it as "the capacity to experience the feelings and understand the thoughts of others." From a neuroscience perspective, empathy is "a complex form of psychological inference that enables us to understand the personal experience of another person through cognitive, evaluative and affective processes."[31] There is, however, a difference between sympathy and empathy. Sympathy means you feel sorry for someone, whereas empathy means you experience what it is like to be someone else.[32]

Film director Ava DuVernay said she first met Roger when she was about eight years old. Her aunt Denise, whom Ava described as a "movie geek," took her to stand outside of the Shrine Auditorium to watch the stars arrive for Oscar rehearsals. Roger walked by and Ava shouted, "Thumbs up!" before he stopped to take a photograph with her. Years later, their encounter came full circle when Ava directed her first film, *I Will Follow*, an homage to her aunt Denise, who used to take her to the movies. Synchronistically, Roger also had an aunt who took him to the movies, his aunt Martha. He related to the feelings the film's protagonist expressed or recognized in others, such as grief, anger, loneliness, confusion, and a sense of being lost for direction, as she cared for a terminally ill loved one. In his review, he noted that he, too, felt and grappled with these same complex emotions. Roger encouraged Ava in her filmmaking and gave the movie a personalized thumbs-up: three and a half stars and a proclamation that it was an invitation to empathy. "It can't have a traditional three-act structure, because every life closes in death, and only supporting characters are left on stage at the end," he said.[33] Ava's review was one that Roger had written after he had already begun facing medical challenges. Reading his reviews from that time, I feel even greater empathy for him, because I recognize more deeply the poignancy he was expressing. These were not simply film reviews to him but a sharing of his soul.

Ava has become one of the most important people in the film world, in my opinion, because of her generosity in passing along that empathy to others. She has single-handedly reached back to bring other filmmakers along with her, especially Black women and people of color. She works to expand access—both in front of and behind the camera—for filmmakers who have traditionally been denied opportunity. Her empathy-driven mission is one she continued to honor in her 2014 movie, *Selma*. In the film, she carefully allows us to see and feel empathy for all Americans who marched and died in the civil rights movement, no matter their race. RogerEbert.com film critic Odie Henderson gave the film four stars and said it announced the arrival of a major talent in Ava, stating, "'Selma' is as much about the procedures of political maneuvering, in-fighting and bargaining as it is about the chief orchestrator of the resulting deals. 'Selma' affords Dr. Martin Luther King Jr. the same human characteristics of humor, frustration, and exhaustion that 'Lincoln' provided its President. This relatable humanity elevates King's actions and his efforts. It inspires by suggesting that the reverence for Dr. King was bestowed on a person not different than any of us. If he can provoke change, we have no excuse not to as well."[34]

Many of us appreciate that Dr. Martin Luther King Jr. was a great man, but seeing his life on the screen, as portrayed by actor David Oyelowo, opens our eyes to how he did not get up, put on a cape in the morning, and acquire superpowers that no one else had. In watching his story play out, we come to admire him even more. Each day Dr. King had to get up and face the same realities we all do, and he had no more tools at his disposal than any one of us do. It was his determination and passion for justice and his love for his family, neighbors, and country that propelled him forward. He did not always know the right thing to do, but he knew that his heart was right and that the people, principles, and laws he was marching for were right. These pillars gave him the motivation to keep fighting the good fight. Watching *Selma* revealed others who had this same level of passion for justice, leading us to truly think that if they could do it, why can't we?

It doesn't have to be a movie about social justice to entice us to put ourselves in the place of a character on the screen. Another stunning display of empathy is visible in the beautifully animated 2015 Pixar film *Inside Out*. I thought the filmmakers (director Pete Docter and cowriters Meg LeFauve and Josh Cooley) were clever to literally provide a window into the emotions of eleven-year-old Riley as she battled the sadness of having to relocate with her family. By showing a panel filled with buttons labeled for each of Riley's emotions—Joy, Sadness, Fear, Disgust, Anger—and characters at the controls of each of those emotions, we could see how one real-life action or event affected everything Riley said and did. When Riley became depressed, we, the audience, felt it too. The visual manifestation of emotion was so palpable on the screen in the way she sat and in her total lack of interest in things. We could see her fear that the rest of her life was destined to be miserable! When I watched this film, I was in a screening room full of grown men and I could hear them holding back sobs. It was not quite what they had expected from a cartoon! When Riley emerged from her sadness, so did we as the viewers. How could this be? The filmmakers said they consulted with psychologists and neuroscientists to construct as accurate a portrayal of our mind and emotions as possible. It worked. Empathy personified.

Roger saw movies as a means of helping us to identify with the people who are sharing this life journey with us. And that, to him, was the most noble thing that movies could do. "We are all born with a certain package. We are who we are. Where we were born, who we were born as, how we were raised. We are kind of stuck inside that person, and the purpose of civilization and growth is to be able to reach out and empathize a little bit with other people, find out what makes them tick, what they care about," he once said.[35] If a film wasn't going to be candid and transparent, allowing full access into someone else's world and providing an authentic view of reality, he felt it wasn't worth making. He wanted to know the heart and soul of the person or matter, and he didn't care much for "puff pieces" or glossed-over filmmaking. His view was that a "sanitized" film wasn't worth the effort, either, because the things that touched people's hearts were the grittier parts, the human parts. He used to say that what made him cry in a movie or in life was not when something is sad but when something or someone is good. His take on movies was more or less an encapsulation of his philosophy of life. I don't know where or when he learned it, but empathy became a lifelong guiding philosophy for him. The passion, care, and curiosity he had for other people is one of the main reasons I chose to be his wife. His concern for the human condition was sincere and profound. I used to tease him, saying that it was so ironic his title was that of "critic," because his core fundamental beliefs were built on walking in another person's shoes to gain enough knowledge to connect with and help them. To him, great movies made us more decent people.

As human beings, we have an undeniable need for connection and want others to see our humanity. These needs are met through empathy.

Part of the culture of the United States and the world is undoubtedly mirrored in movies. Although movies are not meant to be history lessons or even documented studies in life, it is nevertheless vital that what they show and the conversations they depict reflect that we are all in this thing called life together. Empathy is simply the most powerful instrument for social change because if you can feel, even just for a moment, what it's like to be a person of a different age, race, physical ability, or economic circumstance, you can develop the empathy and compassion to act in the care and best interest of the other person . . . which ends up being in the best interest of society as well. I am you and you are me. We all have something to give, and we can all lean in to listen.

No Other

IN THE MANY DECADES of the past, there have been far too many tragic events that have clearly marked those of a different race as "the other," with one of the most notable tragedies being the murder of Emmett Till on August 28, 1955. Emmett was a young boy growing up in a working-class neighborhood on the South Side of Chicago in the 1950s. He was fourteen when his mother let him visit relatives in Money, Mississippi, for the summer. On August 24, 1955, Emmett entered a Money country store while his young cousins, Simeon Wright and Wheeler Parker Jr., waited outside for him. Emmett had intended to buy candy, but reportedly he whistled at a white woman, twenty-one-year-old Carolyn Bryant, as she sat behind the counter. Emmett's mother, Mamie Till-Mobley, doubted this story. She explained that because Emmett had a stutter, she taught him to whistle to get his words unstuck when he spoke. Sadly, there were no witnesses in the store that day to verify what had happened.[36]

In the late night or early morning hours of August 28, Roy Bryant, the store's proprietor and Carolyn's husband, went with his half brother J. W. Milam to the home of Emmett's great-uncle Mose Wright. Roy and J. W. were enraged and looking for Emmett. In spite of Mose's pleas, the two men found the young boy and forced him into their car. Three days later, Emmett's disfigured and brutally beaten body rose from the depths of the Tallahatchie River. Local authorities wanted to bury the body quickly, but Emmett's mother asked that her son's remains be sent back to Chicago. Mamie Till-Mobley was deeply grieved, but she did not want her son's death to be in vain, so she made the decision to have his badly mutilated body viewed in an open casket. She said she wanted the world to see what they had done to her son. *Jet*, the popular African American magazine founded by John Johnson, was the first to publish a photo of Emmett's corpse. Soon after, the mainstream media began to follow. Emmett Till's wake and funeral were held in Chicago over several days in early September 1955 at the Roberts Temple

Church of God in Christ. Estimates of the number of people who attended either his wake or funeral were over one hundred thousand.[37] Despite the evidence against them, Roy Bryant and J. W. Milam were acquitted of murder by an all-white male jury after only sixty-seven minutes of deliberation.[38] They later admitted their guilt in a story in *Look* magazine in January 1956.[39]

Emmett Till's murder and trial gained international attention, and Mamie Till-Mobley's brave action in displaying the brutality of her son's beating spurred the nation to focus on the horrors of racial inequality in the South in a way that had not happened before. People had talked about racial inequality and lynching, but this was a seminal moment that starkly outlined the inequities. It evoked a new national sense of empathy, telegraphed at a time when the population relied on radio, television, and word of mouth for a message to spread. Mamie Till-Mobley's courage in not letting the world forget her son was a galvanizing moment in the civil rights movement and helped to erase that line between "the other" for that moment in history. The purity and ferocity of her love for her son allowed thousands to share in her pain. Rosa Parks later said she was thinking about Emmett and Mamie Till-Mobley when she refused to give up her seat to a white man on the bus in Montgomery, Alabama, on December 1, 1955.[40] Sixty-seven years later, on March 29, 2022, President Joe Biden signed the Emmett Till Antilynching Act, making lynching a federal hate crime.[41]

Empathy digs deep into the best parts of us, helping us to advance the evolution of civilization.

In his contributions to the science of evolution, Charles Darwin stated, "As man advances in civilisation, and small tribes are united into larger communities, the simplest reason would tell each individual that he ought to extend his social instincts and sympathies to all the members of the same nation, though personally unknown to him. This point being once reached, there is only an artificial barrier to prevent his sympathies extending to the men of all nations and races. If, indeed, such men are separated from him by great differences in appearance or habits, experience unfortunately shews us how long it is, before we look at them as our fellow-creatures."[42] Pinpointing the power of empathy (then termed "sympathy"), he wrote, "Those communities, which included the greatest number of the most sympathetic members, would flourish best."[43] Most of us may know Darwin for his work in the theory of how all creatures descended from a small number of original species and how individual animals were marked with variations, some of which allowed those creatures to better survive in their environment. With a greater chance for survival came the opportunity to reproduce and grow. So when we think about Charles Darwin, we often think of his theory of "survival of the fittest." We don't necessarily connect Darwin to empathy, yet his underlying message was about just that—how empathy (then "sympathy") can lead to a more flourishing society. Without empathy, there cannot be survival; as Darwin put it, "This virtue, one of the noblest with which man is endowed, seems to arise incidentally from our sympathies becoming more tender and more widely diffused, until they are extended to all sentient beings. As soon as this virtue is honoured and practised by some few men, it spreads through instruction and example to the young, and eventually becomes incorporated in public opinion."[44] It is a vision that could be equated to "survival of the empathetic."

It is only by putting ourselves in someone else's shoes that we realize we are one.

Our world continues to be in need of greater empathy. We see the lack of such empathy and connection reflected in aspects of politics, families, society, and industry. In 2011, President Barack Obama declared the "empathy deficit" more critical than even the federal deficit.[45] We continue to witness this deficit today, as so many walk through life feeling a sense of emotional isolation. Psychologists Zaki and Cikara state that "empathy is critical for social functioning, but it often wanes when it is needed most." They added that, accordingly, "conflict-reduction interventions prioritize developing empathy in order to achieve harmony."[46]

Mamie Till-Mobley's bold actions served as an intervention of sorts, as they managed to stir society's empathy at a tenuous time when rampant discrimination could have indeed resulted in empathic failure.

Can those of different racial, political, religious, and ideological views learn to come together today and find common ground through empathy? Can we get a group of Fox News watchers at a table with a group of MSNBC watchers and have them find parallels? If we could, what rules would we follow and what would we expect to come from such an exchange? How will we know whether it is successful? And ultimately, is it worth it? Yes, I believe it is possible and that it would result in greater unity, though only when we choose to lead with empathy. Through film and other media, we are helping to move things in the direction of love, unity, and empathy every day, and we are witnessing positive change, new positions, and progressive stories. African American television producer Shonda Rhimes is a great example of this.

She made a big impression on people in Hollywood and around the country when she said she doesn't see herself as someone who embraces "diversity"—she calls it "normalizing."[47] In other words, her writing reflects the normal diversity she experiences in everyday life. She believes that people who write in the entertainment field need to mirror our society.

Discrimination did not end on the day that Mamie Till-Mobley openly showed the world the brutality her son had experienced, but her powerful example of a mother's love and bravery caused journalists to become more empathetic in their storytelling, resulting in telling the truth about lynching instead of covering it up. The survival of our species is not possible without empathy, and every act that evokes and shares it—that portrays it in our news and entertainment—is a step forward in the direction of unity.

This Is Not New Blood

ON MAY 25, 2020, America and the world witnessed forty-six-year-old African American George Floyd suffocate to death in Minneapolis as officer Derek Chauvin knelt on his neck for nine minutes, twenty-nine seconds during an arrest.[48] In his last moments, as he lay face down, handcuffed, pleading for his life, Floyd repeatedly gasped: "I can't breathe." His was an expression of desperation that resonated deeply with parts of the American population, who for far too long felt as though they couldn't breathe or speak their truth. What followed was the rapid and fierce outbreak of global protests inspired by the organization Black Lives Matter. George Floyd's death became another seminal moment of empathy, when people of all colors, ages, genders, lifestyles, and backgrounds came together to demand change for those who have been isolated and whose voices have been repressed. As images of George Floyd's lifeless body began flooding the airwaves and internet, people came out of lockdown in earnest, as this was during pandemic times, and began pleading with vigor to be heard. The rush of subsequent protests and unrest across America and the globe in the mid-2020s felt like a flashback to the 1960s. The wrongful deaths of Breonna Taylor, Philando Castile, Laquan McDonald, Sandra Bland, and far too many others preceded Floyd's. As Martin Luther King Jr. said in his "The Other America" speech in 1967, "Our nation's summers of riots are caused by our nation's winters of delay. And as long as America postpones justice, we stand in the position of having these recurrences of violence and riots over and over again. Social justice and progress are the absolute guarantors of riot prevention."[49]

In August 2019, the *New York Times* ran a series called "The 1619 Project" that surprisingly ignited a backlash against racial empathy. The series was headed by journalist and professor Nikole Hannah-Jones. The title referred to the date more than four hundred years ago when the first ship carrying enslaved Africans landed on the shores of Virginia.[50]

The series was written in an effort to reframe the way we see the institution of slavery and its consequences, as slavery is integral to the understanding of American history, including the shaping of laws that may have bearing on the attitudes of society to this day. It was proposed that the 1619 Project become a part of school curriculum. Some of the backlash resulted from confusion between this project and critical race theory, which is an interdisciplinary field analyzing the intersectionality of race and laws, usually studied in more advanced academic settings such as colleges, universities, and graduate schools. Then, in September 2020, President Donald Trump signed the Executive Order on Combating Race and Sex Stereotyping during a celebration of American history and formed the 1776 Commission to advise on how America's founding story should be taught in schools.[51] That order would presumably make the teaching of the 1619 Project or critical race theory illegal, and would serve as the basis for defunding any educational or business institution that did so. Florida governor Ron DeSantis also championed a bill in his state's legislature, H.B. 7, that would in essence prohibit inflicting discomfort or guilt about one's race. According to the governor's official website, the bill is intended to "give businesses, employees, children and families tools to stand up against discrimination and woke indoctrination."[52]

Empathy is neither automatic nor universal in all situations, especially across racial or political lines.

In his memoir, *Life Itself*, Roger talks about how he grew up in central Illinois having only a few African Americans in his school, and none in his immediate neighborhood. He said the Black students and white students didn't hang out together all the time, and that, from the time he became aware of race, a lot of the opinions he'd formed in his mind were based on books he read including Ralph Ellison's *Invisible Man* and Richard Wright's *Native Son*. As an only child, Roger had to learn to reach out to people and bring them into his playground. He developed this skill so well that you'd think he innately knew how to invite people to the party, including people of other races. He said he specifically asked to be assigned to a university in South Africa as an exchange student so that he could observe the relationships between people of different races. But he never approached the concept as if to say, "Oh, this is something outside of myself," nor did he ever imply he was particularly progressive for doing so. For him, it was just about how you treat another human being, regardless of background or race.

While watching *Life Itself*, I learned something that confirmed what I thought I knew about Roger after all the years we spent together. It was in the scene about his reporting in the *Daily Illini* student newspaper on the four little girls who were murdered in the bombing of the church in Birmingham, Alabama, in 1963. He wrote, "'The blood of these innocent children is on your hands,' Dr. Martin Luther King, Jr. cried out to the governor of Alabama. But that was not entirely the truth. The blood is on so many hands that history will weep in the telling. And it is not new blood. It is old, so very old, and as Lady Macbeth discovered, it will not ever wash away. It clings and it waits and in its turn it kills again." At the time, Roger's means of communicating was through his student newspaper. He very much believed in the power of the press to exhort for justice and for the healthy exchange of ideas. As a student of literature, he thought it was best to imprint the importance of what he was saying about race by tying it to Shakespearean literature. Roger's words were so powerful and he was so young. I wondered where all his empathy came from. I had never read that article, nor had I heard anybody talk about it. And in all the years I knew him, he had never referenced it. When I saw it on film, I was stunned and very impressed that his belief in racial justice was not an afterthought but one formed early and apparently nurtured intentionally throughout his life. His college friend (and later influential sportswriter) the late (William) Bill Nack once told me that Roger felt it was his duty to take a strong stand on race and equality, even if he didn't always know the best way to do it.

Stories—science fiction, comedies, tales about social impact—give us an opportunity to consider and spread positive principles such as forgiveness, empathy, compassion, and kindness.

As we look back on the events of 2020 and beyond, we can see that no one was immune to the impact of the global coronavirus outbreak, and, likewise, we are not immune to the protests or realities tied to human injustice. George Floyd's death served as a catalyst for turning up the volume exponentially on a cry for empathy, equality, and accountability. It was a painful reality in a society where it can feel easier to turn away from anything having to do with racial tensions, disability, illness, death, or other kinds of suffering, unless it hits us personally. There is a bigger societal role in making empathy more universal, and we all play a part. As seen with the media rallying around Mamie Till-Mobley's valiant actions, through good storytelling and empathetic efforts change *can* begin to happen when we come together.

For instance, in my lifetime, I never expected that I would see acts such as the Confederate flag being banned at all NASCAR races and events, yet that is precisely what happened on June 10, 2020. It was two days after Bubba Wallace, the only full-time African American driver in NASCAR, called for the flag's removal. He said, "No one should feel uncomfortable when they come to a NASCAR race."[53] Bubba never set out to be an activist, but he paid attention to what his heart was telling him after the death of George Floyd. He was a race car driver and loved being associated with NASCAR racing. Advocating against an aspect of his sport that caused him pain and that he felt prevented other African Americans from fully embracing the sport required him to step outside his comfort zone.

The Confederate flag has long stood for a time when our nation was torn by a civil war between the North and the South over the issue of slavery. Some justified its existence as a sign of states' rights, or Southern pride, whereas others saw it as an outdated emblem of racial oppression. It is an ancient relic of a war on our soil between our own citizens. Its existence has been a source of suffering throughout generations, and many have long fought against using the flag as a symbol because of its divisive nature. When Bubba Wallace took a stand, something about his actions caused other drivers and spectators alike to pay attention in a way they had not done before. When other people were able to empathize and feel his pain, the resistance to retiring that flag quickly crumbled. In one fell swoop, a paradigm change occurred. What was especially poignant was seeing Bubba Wallace welcomed back to the racetrack after the flag was removed, surrounded by fellow racers who stood with him and drove alongside his car in solidarity. We cannot change the past, though through the act of empathy and by erasing the lines we have been taught to put around anyone perceived as "the other," we can help shape a better future. That is the power of empathy.

Leaning In to Listen

IN AUGUST 2016, San Francisco 49ers quarterback Colin Kaepernick refused to stand during the playing of the national anthem at three preseason games. Instead, he took a knee (meaning he knelt down on one knee), as a means of protest against social injustice and incidents of police brutality. Kaepernick told NFL media in an exclusive interview after the game, "To me, this is bigger than football and it would be selfish on my part to look the other way. There are bodies in the street and people getting paid leave and getting away with murder."[54] After the death of George Floyd in 2020, other NFL players, as well as players in different professional sports, also began taking a knee in protest. Finally, NFL president Roger Goodell spoke out, apologizing and saying that the league was "wrong for not listening to NFL players earlier and encourage all to speak out and peacefully protest."[55] It seemed to many that no one had truly taken the time to understand why Colin Kaepernick had spearheaded the movement of taking a knee during the national anthems.

In August 2020, during an interview with Emmanuel Acho on the *Uncomfortable Conversations with a Black Man* show, Roger Goodell was asked what he'd say to Kaepernick if given the chance. "The first thing I'd say is I wish we had listened earlier, Kaep, to what you were kneeling about and what you were trying to bring attention to." He admitted that he did not know what was going on in the communities and said it was "horrific" to see Floyd's death, along with the subsequent protests against police brutality and racial injustice across the country and around the world. "There was a part of me that said, 'I hope people realize that's what the players were protesting, and that's what's been going on in our communities. You see it now on television, but that's been going on for a long, long time.' And that's where we should have listened sooner," he said. "And we should have been in there with them." He admitted that the NFL alone couldn't solve all problems, though they have a platform in their communities, which means they have an opportunity. He indicated that the league would be using that platform for good now, though he wished they would have been doing so earlier.[56]

Empathy is a skill, not a fixed mindset or innate ability.

Australian philosopher Roman Krznaric is the author of the internationally bestselling book *Empathy: Why It Matters, and How to Get It* and the founder of the world's first Empathy Museum and the digital Empathy Library. Anyone can become a part of the series of participatory art projects at his traveling museum. The organization's objective is to help people look at the world through other people's eyes. With a focus on storytelling and dialogue, the museum explores how empathy can not only transform our personal relationships but also help tackle global challenges such as prejudice, conflict, and inequality. The establishment's best-known project is called *A Mile in My Shoes*, and it features a giant shoebox filled with row upon row of other people's footwear. Participants can quite literally step into someone else's shoes! For a few moments in time, anyone can put on the sandals of a Syrian refugee or the heels of a sex worker, while listening to a recording of that person speaking about his or her life and experiences. The exhibit has already been to the United Kingdom, Belgium, Ireland, the United States, Australia, Brazil, and Siberia.[57]

Krznaric points out that a greater understanding of empathy is in order. He states, "Empathy doesn't stop developing in childhood. We can nurture its growth throughout our lives—and we can use it as a radical force for social transformation." His work with the Empathy Museum and beyond is helping global audiences understand its importance and see it as a skill that can be cultivated, especially with greater research and guidance. In his words, "The big buzz about empathy stems from a revolutionary shift in the science of how we understand human nature. The old view that we are essentially self-interested creatures is being nudged firmly to one side by evidence that we are also *homo empathicus*, wired for empathy, social cooperation, and mutual aid. Over the last decade, neuroscientists have identified a ten-section 'empathy circuit' in our brains which, if damaged, can curtail our ability to understand what other people are feeling."[58] Based on his research showing that empathy is a habit we can cultivate to improve the quality of our lives, it is clear that we all have a natural capacity for empathy. By consciously embracing the habits of attentiveness, care, curiosity, and nonjudgment, we can develop the empathy muscle already present within each of us.

Empathy is about attentiveness and intention, as well as science. Neuroscientists have discovered that, through our mirror neurons, our limbic system can be activated both by observation of others in pain and by firsthand experience of physical pain. Studies have shown that people who identify as more empathic have stronger activations both in the mirror system, providing more direct support for the idea that the mirror system is linked to empathy.[59] But Zaki and Cikara remind us of a frequent misimpression about empathy: "One common assumption is that empathy is uncontrollable—something that automatically happens or does not happen to perceivers when they encounter others in distress." This is to say that we falsely believe we cannot develop empathy. They state, "Because conflict-related emotions are characterized by both the absence of compassion and the presence of antipathy, parties in active conflict should focus on regulating these emotions prior to social encounters."[60]

When it comes to what we can do to increase empathy, Zaki and Cikara explain that conflict-reduction interventions could still be improved with a more nuanced understanding of empathy. First, empathy is a multidimensional construct, including understanding, sharing, and feeling concern for others' emotions. The expression of these empathic processes is further influenced by psychological factors that "tune" people toward or away from empathy. Interventions must therefore diagnose the specific nature and precursors of empathic failures and tailor interventions appropriately. Second, empathy alone may be insufficient to produce prosocial behavior, especially when parties differ in status or power. In these cases, interventions should promote equitable goals and norms in addition to empathy. By understanding its component processes and boundary conditions, practitioners can work to promote empathy in maximally effective ways.[61] The conclusion of their research was that "empathy often appears to be in short supply, especially during interpersonal and intergroup conflict. Resulting apathy and antipathy stand in the way of peace building and conflict resolution. However, simply fostering more empathy may not always facilitate positive change. Therefore, addressing lapses in empathy—as well as the boundary conditions of empathy itself—should constitute a key mission not only of social scientists but of practitioners and policymakers as well."[62]

Empathy is a visceral feeling with the power to inextricably bind us to one another.

Shortly after Colin Kaepernick took a knee during the national anthem, I had an experience that really got me thinking. A friend and fellow member of a global women's group concerned with health research and philanthropy shared her thoughts of his actions with me, saying she believed what he had done was horrible and that he should be kicked off the team for dishonoring the flag and the nation. Her comment caught me off guard, as in our four years of friendship I had always perceived her to be kind, compassionate, and lighthearted. Whenever our group took trips, she and I would be the ones dashing up a mountain together in Argentina or planning to have our families meet if we happened to be in a foreign country at the same time. We'd also discussed the plight of women without adequate health care or children who didn't have resources for advanced education and plotted solutions that could help. We were both claustrophobic, so we found ourselves sitting in the front seat together in rental vans or in the most open spaces at restaurants. We spent a lot of time in each other's company on those trips. In addition to being compassionate and kind, she was very funny, and we often found ourselves laughing at some odd situation. Ironically, we'd never spoken about each other's politics.

That day when she asked if I felt the same way about Colin Kaepernick, I told her I did not.

I shared that I believed his actions were not against the flag but were rather his patriotic way of saying that he was not going to honor tradition because he opposed the actions that oppress Black people and people of color. I had listened to Colin Kaepernick's rationale and knew he felt as though he were waging a peaceful protest using his privileged platform to speak out. Following our exchange, my friend and I did not converse for quite some time. I dreaded our women's group coming together because of the emotional discomfort I anticipated we would each feel. I was reluctant to see her, and I assumed she was reluctant to see me. I didn't know how we would feel about each other, given our widely differing views on this highly publicized event.

During our friendship hiatus, I spoke with a mutual friend about the disagreement, trying to gain perspective on my friend's position. In that exchange, I learned about her political background and other causes with which she was involved. I tried to put myself in her shoes. Did I really think the person I had been friends with for four years had changed that much overnight? I'd always found her to be compassionate and warm. Did her thoughts about

Kaepernick make her less so? But down to the real nitty-gritty, could we be friends with such opposite views? I had other friends and colleagues whose political views I disagreed with, but that was not the sole measure of our friendship. In fact, some of our most entertaining visits in London occurred when Roger and I met up with the novelist and journalist Auberon Waugh at the Academy Club. Waugh, whose politics were decidedly to the right, was smart and funny, and he, Roger, and I conversed easily, while eyeing the other curiously. I pondered all of these issues in earnest because I knew a luncheon was coming up when my friend and I would be face-to-face with each other again.

Then we saw each other for the first time in months, and, to my surprise, her face lit up. And so did mine. We hugged and carried on as if nothing had ever happened. I realized in that moment that sometimes empathy is about being civil and accepting the differences of others, even when we disagree. As we sat together and enjoyed our lunch, there was no mention of our disagreement, and on that day we did not broach the subject. Regardless of our differing perspectives, I remained confident that I could call on her if I were in need of anything and she could call on me. In life, sometimes there is no one definitive way to relate to another person. There is not always a rule book or game book. Things can get complicated and messy, though when we lead with empathy, we can allow ourselves a much shorter trek through the muck of those complications.

Fast forward to September 2023. Our women's group took a trip to the Basque regions of Spain and France. It had been a couple of years since this friend and I had seen each other. For almost two weeks during the trip we fell right back into our previously friendly ways of greeting each other and catching up on things in the world. I waited until the very last day of the trip to let her know that I was writing about her in this book. She was surprised. She had forgotten about our disagreement over Kaepernick. When I reminded her, we immediately both asked the other if our positions had changed. The answer was no. I still felt that Kaepernick had done what he'd thought was right in protesting actions of inequality. And he'd paid a price for it. Not surprisingly, she still felt he was wrong and that he had disrespected the flag and our soldiers by not standing during the national anthem. What did we do? Did we stomp away in anger or try to change the other's mind? No, we looked at each other—and laughed! Then she said: "I love you even more to know that we can have an open and civil conversation about it, and that it didn't affect the way we feel about each other." And that is exactly the way I felt too. A living example of empathy in action. I sure wish we could teach it to our Congress.

To reduce the frequency of horrific acts in our world, we all need to become proactive with our empathy building... and to build empathy, we have to begin by being willing to forgive. For Roger Goodell, that meant understanding Colin Kaepernick's actions without judgment; for Kaepernick, that meant forgiving any prior lack of action or support from Goodell, knowing that Goodell had done the best he could with what he knew (which he later came to realize was not enough). To begin to elicit and develop true empathy, we can show up for one another, we can listen, and, even if we disagree, we can choose to understand and respect one another's opinions. We can allow ourselves to recognize the pain other people are feeling and put ourselves in their shoes long enough to, at the very least, acknowledge the source of the pain and, in that moment, do what we can to figure out a way to help alleviate it. It doesn't matter whether we gain empathy for others by watching a movie, reading a book, studying history, or having personally experienced a similar slight or pain. The point is to learn to gain that visceral feeling that allows us to act in the best interest of all.

The Beauty of Bridging Worlds

DIRECTOR MARY MAZZIO'S 2017 film, *I Am Jane Doe*, brought the world into a reality where a film can result in the passing of progressive legislation. Mary's work helped strengthen anti–sex trafficking laws in the United States. Then came her 2020 film, *A Most Beautiful Thing*, born from her love for rowing and her ongoing desire to spur social change. Mary had come across a tweet by Arshay Cooper, the captain of the first African American high school rowing team in the US, telling others about his self-published memoir, *A Most Beautiful Thing*. She found his book mesmerizing and his story inspiring, devastating, funny, sad, and hopeful all at the same time. Arshay was the son of a woman struggling with generational trauma and addiction and the brother of gang members. When he discovered rowing, he found something that changed his life and the lives of those he came to call teammates. While pursuing his new passion, "the water provided a backdrop for who and what he could become." It was, as he wrote, "a place where you could not hear the noise of the West Side . . . bullets, sirens . . . and that was a beautiful thing."[63]

When Mary finished reading Arshay's memoir, she tweeted: "Amazing story @ArshayCooper." Within fifteen minutes, a tweet rocketed back: "Thx @MaryMazzio, let's talk." Before she could even reply, her phone rang. It was Arshay calling with a proposal. The dream of turning his book into a film had been born. Within a matter of weeks, Arshay and Alvin Ross, Arshay's teammate and best friend, were picking up Mary from the Chicago O'Hare airport. They handed her a baseball cap, and Alvin turned up "Walk Wit' Me" by local hip-hop artist DA Smart as they drove her to their neighborhood. "You need to hear this," Alvin said. "It's the story of our lives."[64] As someone unfamiliar with the West Side of Chicago, Mary was stunned by the geography of affiliated corners. Different gangs ran the blocks, sometimes one block only, with the next block run by a rival gang. Arshay shared that he felt the area was truly never safe. Growing up, he had barely been able to get to school, because if you passed through a neighborhood where you were not known, you'd get jumped. That was their everyday struggle.

Physically stepping into someone else's world can help us build empathy in a uniquely powerful manner.

After touring the West Side, Mary began to learn about the incredible leadership and training that went into building Arshay's rowing team. She listened during candid discussions with him and his teammates about structural impediments, intergenerational trauma, the toxic relationship with law enforcement, and what it meant to be navigating life in neighborhoods such as the West Side. Arshay became inspired to invite the Chicago Police Department to join them in the indoor rowing tanks, to teach them how to row and to get to know them, though his teammates were hesitant. Mary and her crew were on-site to film the first meeting of the Chicago police and Arshay's team. She described the interchange as extraordinary kindness by Arshay and his teammates toward the officers, as they patiently taught them how to row and as they worked together, shoulder to shoulder. What made it most powerful was that Alvin and Preston, the team's stroke seat, were intimately familiar with the criminal justice system, because they had both been incarcerated.

Mary showed me parts of the film as she was editing it, and I became so interested that I joined the production as an executive producer. It was not an immediate decision, however, as I was wary of the film at first, thinking it could be a story of a "white savior" going into Black neighborhoods to protect us from ourselves. Having grown up on the West Side of Chicago, I was particularly sensitive. As I observed Mary's process, I saw the respect she had for Arshay and all his teammates, and I saw the respect that Arshay and his teammates had for her. Also, Arshay was not one to sit idly back and let someone else tell his story; he was an active participant in forming his narrative. Mary respected the boundaries between her and the subjects of the film. In her words, "These young men invited me into their world, into their realities, reminding me of our collective responsibility for the conditions we (the greater 'we') created and the long shadow of the trauma our ancestors inflicted upon a generation of African-Americans (some call it slavery but the violence endemic in the slave trade makes the term 'slavery' almost quaint. The term really should be 'domestic terrorism')."[65]

A Most Beautiful Thing opened in March 2020, as Mary hoped it would show thought leaders and legislators how much work is needed to level the safety playing field for our children. The film quickly garnered the interest of congressman Danny K. Davis of the Seventh Congressional District in Chicago, who invited Mary to speak before Congress in Washington, DC.

After the coronavirus pandemic caused a cancellation of our scheduled in-person panel for the opening premier of the film, Chicago mayor Lori Lightfoot appeared remotely at a panel I moderated alongside Ms. Mazzio, NBA star Dwayne Wade, former Secretary of Education Arne Duncan, and Michael Strautmanis of the Obama Foundation. The panel was hosted by Comcast, the Chicago

International Film Festival, and the Chicago Film Office. The panelists spoke of the brilliance of Chicagoans who banded together to find healing through community and collective strength and dedication. The documentary was a decided hit in spurring inspired conversation about how to bring about further healing.

Everything that we give in the name of empathy will have real impact.

Once we experience empathy through any medium and circumstance that serves to generate it, and we have put ourselves in someone else's shoes, there are actions to be taken and contributions to be made. Being empathetic alone is not enough. We must *do something*. To me, a documentary such as *A Most Beautiful Thing* models what we can do. It has a timelessness to it, in the way that it speaks to principles with real-world consequences, such as empathy, compassion, and kindness. Arshay's extension of an olive branch—his invitation to police officers to train with them—improved relations between the former gang members and law enforcement. Everything that they undertook also had real impact for them personally. While their rowing team may not have ended up at the Olympics, Arshay's teammates also didn't end up in jail, or dead. Instead, they ended up starting businesses. One of them opened a moving company where he could hire people from the neighborhood; another opened a barbershop, where he taught his own barbershop philosophy. They all became role models for younger members of the community. It was indeed a beautiful thing.

Dealing with the Discomfort

WHEN EMMY-NOMINATED filmmaker, author, and Webby Awards founder Tiffany Shlain[66] and the team at Let It Ripple film studio—a company whose mission is to engage people in conversation and action around complicated subjects that are shaping our lives—set out to identify the skills we need to flourish as people and communities in today's world, they began with a single question: What's a great example of a twenty-first-century mind in action? Their question prompted a host of responses about incredible technological breakthroughs and innovations, along with one story that stood out, opening the door to a new way of thinking. The story was about Mary Beth Heffernan, an art professor in California. While watching news coverage of the 2014–2015 Ebola crisis in West Africa, Mary Beth was struck by the head-to-toe personal protective equipment (PPE) the doctors were wearing. "Wait a second," she thought. "These patients must be so scared and lonely, and the only humans they're seeing are covered in these huge imposing suits." She imagined what it might be like for a patient not to see a single person's face for days on end and realized that maybe she was the one to help reveal those faces. She began studying West African culture as well as the practice of isolating patients from their families as the extreme nature of the virus demanded. When doctors in Liberia welcomed Mary Beth to begin her work in their Ebola clinics, she jumped into action, seeing to it that all healthcare workers affixed a picture of themselves to the front of their hazmat suits. At last, they each had a face.[67] During the 2020 coronavirus outbreak, Robertino Rodriguez, a respiratory therapist at Scripps Mercy Hospital in San Diego, did exactly what Mary Beth had done. He placed a laminated photo of his face and name on his PPE gear. "A reassuring smile makes a big difference to a scared patient. So today I made a giant laminated badge for my PPE. So my patients can see a reassuring and comforting smile," he wrote. Nurses in Los Angeles and other cities soon followed suit.[68]

So many among us walk through our days feeling a great deal of loneliness. Nearly all of us experienced some level of isolation during the COVID-19 pandemic. We never imagined we would see the whole world shut down. Stay-at-home orders and words such as "quarantine" and "self-isolation" became a part of our daily vocabulary. Businesses and schools had to adapt to operating virtually. The things we once took for granted became things we recognized as truly valuable. Many among us were forced to distance ourselves from friends, family, and loved ones, which left us longing for connection like never before. We were yearning for human warmth, the sound of a voice, the sight of a face, the touch of a handshake, or a good word to make us laugh and feel reassured that we were not alone. We developed the means to reach out and connect with others digitally, though we learned that was not preferable to in-person interaction. Having the opportunity to experience this aloneness for ourselves gave us the empathy to imagine the desolation that others who live without much emotional connection must feel—people such as those in nursing homes or orphanages, or even those estranged from their families.

In a 2014 TEDx Talk titled "The Power & Science of Social Connection," Emma Seppälä, science director of Stanford University's Center for Compassion and Altruism Research and Education, shared that the average number of people to whom we feel close enough to share a personal problem with is two, although the majority of people responded that they had zero confidants. That would equate to one in four Americans who do not feel a close connection with others.[69]

We all deserve to have a voice and a face. We all have something to give. And we can all lean in to listen.

On February 29, 2016, I hosted a dinner for ten African American and Latino high school students whom I mentored through the Columbia College Links Journalism program. We also invited their program administrators and members from the Chicago Urban League, as well as editors from RogerEbert.com. I saw these students as our future. My heart was soaring because they were talking about learning to care more for one another's well-being. These were students from different schools who in the normal course of their lives would have never met. They discussed how watching and writing about movies made them think differently about other people. They said they felt more accepting of people who were different after the films enriched their understanding of the lives of others. The films also helped them identify with other people's challenges and dreams just a bit more.

As we moved on to discussing whether there was value in watching the Academy Awards, their tone changed. "Why should we care? If you don't want to watch it, don't watch it," they said. I urged them to recognize how vitally important it was to watch. As I drilled down in the conversation,

I discovered that underneath part of the seeming antipathy toward the Academy Awards was fear—fear that "those" awards weren't for them and that their thoughts, ideas, and screenplays would never make it to that lofty stage. With millions of people around the world tuning in to the Academy Awards, I explained that they needed to be able to envision themselves (or someone like them) on that screen. They needed to be part of the conversation. Their voices as African American or Latino filmmakers, film critics, or artists should be heard, and their faces should be seen. To be clear, it is OK if someone doesn't want to watch the Academy Awards because it is not their area of interest. But it is a problem if students of color who are interested in film and the arts don't want to watch the Academy Awards because they think they can never aspire to be honored at such a ceremony, as they see it as only for others who are not Black or brown. It surprised me to hear them say this, and it caused me to listen to their hopes, dreams, aspirations, and fears a bit closer. Sometimes empathy is leaning in to really listen to someone else.

It is important not to avoid conversations about gender, race, age, disability, illness, death, or sexuality.

Leslie Jamison, in her 2014 *New York Times* bestselling book *The Empathy Exams*, asks key questions about how we can better understand others. "How can we feel another's pain, especially when pain can be assumed, distorted, or performed?"[70] In the October 2020 *New York Times* article "5 People Who Can Help You Strengthen Your Empathy Muscle," Jamison said that the essential question to be asked when there is so much we don't know about other people's experiences is "What are the small ways I can act on that unknowing?" "Sometimes the greatest extension of empathy," she said, "is to tell somebody that you can't understand what that person is feeling rather than to say something rote, like 'that must be hard.'"[71] Roger said that in his movie reviews he didn't shrink away from talking about the things people saw differently because of race or religion. He was sometimes criticized for this, with some people telling him to stay in his own lane, but we are part of the human race and this is *our* lane. Roger was sincerely curious. He wanted to get along with others. And he knew he didn't possess all the knowledge he needed to do so.

It is my firm belief that diversity, equity, and inclusion determine not only how we see society but how we heal as a larger, global community. We cannot begin the process of healing or changing something until we admit it is a societal aspect in need of our support and attention. We must examine what is wrong and ask what we can do to make it right. It is important not to avoid conversations about gender, race, age, disability, illness, death, or sexuality. We must have these conversations openly. Making a video, sharing a message, or standing up for someone can each be a way to help redress wrongs and show that we give a FECK. We can be open to conversations about how to be an ally—or just generally, what we can do to further a relationship and build greater empathy. Because when we can really feel what it is like to be in another person's situation, it helps us to be more compassionate toward them. We may better understand what acts of kindness can help alleviate their suffering. It helps us to be more forgiving.

"The time is always right to do what is right," said Dr. Martin Luther King Jr.,[72] and we have many ways to build greater empathy every day. We can make films, create narratives, and tell stories that showcase and elicit the transparency advocated by Roger. This empathy in action is about creating better citizens and a stronger community, because every day we continue to witness events where our beliefs divide us, even though all we really want is to be loved and feel connected with one another. It doesn't have to be a big gesture. Having empathy—a key component of the FECK formula—is an opportunity for each of us to establish our own legacy. The following pages contain exercises and questions for you to consider in the name of helping to build greater empathy.

Empathy Journal

Empathy Exercise 1: Choose Your Character

As you learned in this section of the book, empathy is a skill that takes time to develop. Here is a great practice you can use, which can be executed without judgment.

Select a film or book that you believe exhibits the principle of empathy. Identify the main character of the story and consider the following questions.

What is the greatest challenge that character faces?

____

____

____

____

____

____

____

What about this character is different from you?

____

____

____

____

____

What about this character can you relate to?

____

____

____

____

____

What solution did this character apply to resolve a challenge?

____

____

____

____

What lesson did this character learn that you can apply to the real world? ______________________________

____

____

____

____

Empathy Exercise 2: Find the Right Words

When we encounter someone or know someone who is from a very different walk of life or who is going through something we have never experienced, it can be challenging to find the right words to say or the right actions to take. In this chapter's journal, spend time imagining yourself in the A Mile in My Shoes exhibit of the Empathy Museum. Step back from whatever you are doing (or from thinking about what you need to do) and just be with this person or thoughts of this person.

Then complete the following sentences:

When I allow myself to step into this person's shoes, what I begin to see *is . . .* ______________________________

____

____

____

____

____

____

____

____

____

____

When I allow myself to step into this person's shoes, what I begin to feel *at the deepest level is . . .*

____

____

____

____

____

____

When I allow myself to develop greater empathy for this person, it frees me to . . . ____________________

____

____

____

____

____

____

When I allow this empathy building to change our relationship, it permits me/us to . . .

____

____

____

____

____

____

Empathy Exercise 3: Apply Deep Listening

One goal of this book is to make empathetic listening a part of mainstream culture. This chapter's journal entry focuses on exploring where you can apply deep listening to build greater empathy.

One person who is going through something I struggle to understand and with whom I could use empathetic listening to help me see where this person is coming from is . . . ______________________________

____

____

____

____

____

____

In listening deeply to this person, I hope to be able to . . .

____

____

____

____

____

____

____

When this person and I have greater empathy in our relationship, we will be able to . . . ________________

____

____

____

____

____

____

____

____

____

____

FECK PRINCIPLE 3

Compassion

Intentional Action

NONE OF US saw Roger's death coming. There had been no warning that it was imminent. Film director Gregory Nava and his fiancée (now wife) and screenwriting partner, Barbara Martinez, had come to town to attend a musical performance with me at the beginning of April 2013. Midway through *Rigoletto* at the Lyric Opera, I fell asleep (after having spent countless hours at Roger's bedside) and awoke with the awareness of having had a dream that my teeth were loose and falling out. Depending on the cultural association, such a dream can be seen as an omen of loss. Indeed, Barbara had studied at the University of California-Irvine with the dynamic theatre director and performance theorist Jerzy Grotowski. One of her most cherished semesters as a core member of his Objective Drama project was when they studied the actions and rituals of various groups and societies around death. And she confirmed to me that my dream about loose teeth was sometimes interpreted as a harbinger of death in many cultures.

The week following my *Rigoletto* dream, Roger transitioned. But we were not prepared. The plan had been for me to take him home from the Rehabilitation Institute of Chicago for home hospice care, in the hopes of helping him build enough strength for more rehabilitation. He was happy and smiling that morning, as I whispered in his ear, "We're going home." He typed "Home?!" and gave me the thumbs-up, smiling excitedly at me, as his computer-generated voice repeated the word "home." He signaled for me to come to the bed to give him a big hug, and as we finished our embrace, he looked deeply into my eyes. In that moment, I could see his happiness and contentment, which I thought was related to his finally being able to return to the comforts of our own place after another stint in rehabilitation. I hadn't realized that perhaps we each had a different definition of the word "home." He then took his pen and paper and wrote over and over again, "I Love You, I Love You, I Love You." I walked out of the room to allow the nurses to help Roger get dressed to leave. When I walked back in to ask him a question, he looked at me, gave me a joyful beatific smile, and put his head down. We thought he was meditating. He wasn't; he was leaving us. Roger seemed to know he was going to die and he accepted that. If was as if he had stared death right in the eye and said, "I'm not afraid. I'm ready for you. I'm coming."

Gregory and Barbara joined me and my daughter, Sonia Evans, in Roger's room. They sat silently with us, holding my hand, as I held Roger's. We put on some of his favorite Dave Brubeck music and gathered in a circle, saying prayers and doing what we could to help guide his spirit out of this life and into the next one. Director Steve James, who was in the middle of shooting Roger's documentary, came into the Rehabilitation Institute to see him as well, yet it was too late. Steve, immediately respecting the sanctity of the death room and the privacy of our mourning, put his camera down and sat with us in silence. Until I experienced it with Roger, I never expected dying to be so beautiful. The atmosphere in the room when he transitioned was one of love, peace, and serenity. He moved on effortlessly. Watching Roger transition took away any fear of death I ever had. I realized it was time for me to let him go, although I didn't want to at first. I let out a plaintive sob and wanted the medical staff to resuscitate him. But Roger had signed a do not resuscitate order (DNR). I wanted so badly to cut the DNR band off his wrist and hide it, so I could beg them to revive him. Then suddenly, a feeling came over me that was rather unusual. It was as though a soothing warm honey were spreading through my veins and with it came a powerful acceptance of Roger's wishes. With a big sigh, I exhaled. Letting him go peacefully was the right thing to do. It was the loving, compassionate thing to do. I wanted to make it as effortless and heavenly for him as possible.

It is the heart's truest desire to take intentional, loving action for another person or for a group of people.

Emma Seppälä of the Center for Compassion and Altruism Research and Education differentiates between compassion and empathy:

> What is compassion and how is it different from empathy or altruism? The definition of compassion is often confused with that of empathy. Empathy, as defined by researchers, is the visceral or emotional experience of another person's feelings. It is, in a sense, an automatic mirroring of another's emotion, like tearing up at a friend's sadness. Altruism is an action that benefits someone else. It may or may not be accompanied by empathy or compassion, for example in the case of making a donation for tax purposes. Although these terms are related to compassion, they are not identical. Compassion often does, of course, involve an empathic response and an altruistic behavior. However, compassion is defined as the emotional response when perceiving suffering and involves an authentic desire to help.[73]

The day Roger passed away, I was immediately surrounded by so many compassionate people, from my daughter, Sonia, to the medical staff at the Rehabilitation Institute of Chicago, to director Gregory Nava and his fiancée, Barbara Martinez, and director Steve James. Thea Flaum, Carolyn Chambless, Marlene McGuirt, Liza Antelo, and other longtime friends let me know that I would not be alone. Even those people with whom I had only recently established business relationships were extending a helping hand. My relatively new attorneys, Joe Ginsburg and Morris Saunders, stepped forward and helped me figure out all the things I had not thought of, such as deciding which funeral home to call, canceling the home hospice care, and coordinating arrangements between the Rehabilitation Institute and the ambulance service. We didn't have any of those details worked out in advance, because we really thought Roger would return to our house and that he would have at least another two years to live. When Joe stepped in, it was more as a father figure than a lawyer. Alongside him, Eliot Ephraim, our longtime attorney, arrived to help receive documents that I was in no position to review. My daughter, Sonia, knew how much I was suffering and continued to be my rock, even as she was anticipating how difficult it would be to break the news about Grandpa Roger to the grandchildren who loved him so much.

When I look back on the period after losing Roger, I don't know how I got through everything. I had no idea where to begin, and it was all too much to think about. The universe obviously had a plan for me, as so many angels began to show up in my life. I experienced true compassion from so many people. What stands out even today is the emotional warmth and genuine care they extended to me. No task was too large or too small for anyone to execute; they just wanted to do whatever they could to help me and, by extension, Roger. Their every word and gesture felt authentic. They let me know that I was not alone.

In the days that followed, I was stunned at how quickly word got out about Roger's death. An announcement of his passing had been broadcast on the radio while he transitioned, even before we had left his bedside! To ensure that Roger was being honored in the way we wanted him to be, Joe called our new public-relations people, and Robin Beaman and Shawn Taylor rushed over to help us deal with the media. They worked to make sure my statement to the public reflected my own personal sentiment. "What do you want people to know about your life with Roger?" Joe asked me. "My prince is dead" were the first words that came out of my mouth. "But I want them to know how grateful I am for the lovely, lovely life we had together. It was more epic than any movie." And Mary Kellogg, Don DuPree, the former director of Roger's television show, as well as Larry Dieckhaus, Janet LaMonica, David Plummer, Stuart Cleland, and others from the show, also called, came by, and offered to do everything they could to assist. They were so very helpful. They had always admired both Roger and Gene Siskel.

Calls started coming in from all over the world, and Greg and Barbara put all their Hollywood meetings on hold to stay in Chicago and help me prepare Roger's memorial services. Yvonne McNair, one of my daughter's best friends since junior high in Naperville, had her own events company and went to work orchestrating a private funeral service for Roger at Holy Name Cathedral, separate from the public memorial service to be held at the Chicago Theatre. Roger's longtime producer from the local ABC station, Marsha Jordan, helped provide footage for the service, from the years that Roger had broadcast for Disney from their studios.

Right before Roger's memorial service, I began to feel pressure in my chest. Joe made an appointment for me with my personal physician and drove me to the hospital. After the appropriate tests, I learned that my symptoms were induced by stress. Joe stood by my side and constantly reaffirmed to me that he and all the others were there for me. Their compassion and kindness left me feeling supported and protected. I began receiving cards from around the world with notes that made me smile. There was the group of friends who insisted on taking me out for dinner even when I had no appetite, because they knew I needed to eat. During those first few days, when I was hardly sleeping, a friend called Sonia and made arrangements to have a massage therapist come to the house. Some even answered my personal phone so I wouldn't have to continue repeating the same thing to everyone who called. My good friend Nancy Koppelman flew in from Montecito to collect the flowers and UPS packages arriving at the house, placing all her personal appointments on hold to stay in Chicago to help. (And when she later passed away from cancer in 2017, I was able to reciprocate by helping to plan and officiate at her memorial service.)

I would like to also say thank you to a few others who were so compassionate and caring both during Roger's illness and after he passed away: Oprah Winfrey, Richard Roeper, Michael Barker, the copresident of Sony Pictures Classics, studio head Sherry Lansing and her husband, the late, great director William Friedkin, and, most surprisingly, Howard Stern, whose level of compassion and seriousness all throughout Roger's illness truly touched my heart. There were so many others from the worlds of academia, filmmaking, film criticism, and our daily lives who reached out to offer to do anything they could. The names are too numerous to mention, but I want you to know, it all helped me to get through that very sad and painful period. Thanks also to Chris Tucker, who sat with me, expressing his concern and providing comfort during Roger's memorial service at the Chicago Theatre.

When we can deeply and accurately understand other people's challenges, only then can we understand how to contribute to alleviating their suffering and raising their spirits.

When I was with Roger in his final months, those who helped us didn't always ask us what we needed. In their deep compassion, they looked around to see what could help us the most, and they took the initiative to identify what we were going to need. The acts of compassion I received are what helped me get out of bed in the mornings, when most days I felt like pulling the blankets over my head. I remain forever grateful to all who stepped in to lend a hand. When we choose to operate with empathy and compassion, they work together because we are watching and anticipating the needs of another. Then we act on those needs to help alleviate suffering and raise spirits, whether someone knows what to ask for or not. Compassion ultimately happens when we listen to our intuition and when we ask how we can help or proactively take action that we know will help others, even when they are unable to articulate their needs. Our caring about others makes us willing to lend a hand. As Emma Seppälä writes, "Suffering, as unpleasant as it is, often also has a bright side to which research has paid less attention: compassion. Human suffering is often accompanied by beautiful acts of compassion by others wishing to help relieve it."[74]

The day of Roger's funeral, Matt Fagerholm, one of our RogerEbert.com editors, told me that he and others began lining up outside the church at 3:00 a.m. to pay their respects to Roger. Later, when I asked him why, Matt said: "If you were a painter and you heard that Monet died, or a musician and Mozart died, you would get there at 3:00 a.m. to pay your respects. Roger, within the world of films and film criticism, had that same impact."

A Constant Process

DURING THE MANY WEEKS that Roger spent in the hospital over the course of his illness, I would remain by his bedside for hours. One day, I was sitting next to him postsurgery as he lay there sleeping. All I could focus on was the oppressiveness of the room's four walls and the bombardment of hospital smells. It was suffocatingly warm, and I was feeling overwhelmed. Dr. Pelzer, Roger's oncologist, and Dr. Havey, his personal physician, advised me to get up and go outside just to take a walk and clear my head. They knew it wasn't easy for me to leave Roger's side, but they advocated a bit of self-care during a situation they reminded me was a marathon, not a sprint. Both doctors exhibited compassion and care that went beyond mechanical medical care. Throughout Roger's ordeal they were truly angels in our midst.

On June 18, 2013, the day that would have been Roger's seventy-first birthday, I was invited to help bestow Dr. Peltzer with the Gary A. Mecklenburg Distinguished Physician Award at Northwestern Memorial Hospital. The award is presented to a physician, nominated by his or her peers, "who embodies professionalism and humanism" and who demonstrates "a strong commitment to enriching the lives of others through research, teaching, patient care or community outreach."[75] Dr. Peltzer was Roger's lead oncology surgeon at Northwestern Memorial Hospital in Chicago. Roger said that Dr. Pelzer was quite simply one of the finest human beings he had ever met. He and his team, including Dr. Robert Havey and Dr. Neil Fine, worked around the clock providing Roger with some of the finest medical care available. They were all smart, well-trained doctors, but Roger said it was their compassion that made him feel like a human being and not just a "lump on a hospital bed."

Despite being in great demand at the hospital, Dr. Peltzer would make time to sit by Roger's bedside and listen to our fears. He continually went out of his way to do more than was medically necessary, even helping Roger shave for the first time in weeks when he regained his ability to do so. Dr. Peltzer always seemed to have the right words to uplift us emotionally. This respected surgeon took a complete and holistic approach to healing the whole of a patient's psyche. I later learned he did the same for many of his other patients! We all idolized him, and he exuded a gentle, caring bedside manner that always brought me to tears. And Dr. Havey did the same. He listened, he researched, and he came back with care and compassion. I am not surprised that someone has endowed the Robert J. Havey, MD, Institute for Global Health at the Northwestern University Feinberg School of Medicine. And I hope that Dr. Pelzer finally gets some department with the word "Compassion" in it. The same can be said for Dr. James Sliwa and the late Dr. Joann Smith at the Rehabilitation Institute of Chicago (now the Shirley Ryan AbilityLab). These physicians treated the whole human being, not just the sick patient. Dr. Sliwa later told me that the Shirley Ryan AbilityLab established an area of rehabilitation that focused on preparing the patient for reentry into a more productive work life based partially on things he observed in Roger during that period. He saw how integral Roger's work had been in speeding his healing process. That it was so important in helping to give Roger the motivation to write, live, go to the opera, be present for our grandchildren, and be there for his readers and those who communicated with him on social media in the last years of his life. I am so very grateful for the extraordinary medical care he received from these top-notch physicians.

For both Roger and me, facing a host of health challenges together was like living in a foreign land where you didn't speak the language, recognize the food, or know the customs. What I also learned was that when facing a situation that is life-or-death, it's incredible how quickly we forget to offer ourselves compassion. In supporting Roger, I learned that I had to show compassion not only to him but also to myself, because we were living the journey together. Having compassionate doctors and leaders around helped me remember to be more self-compassionate, and when I was more self-compassionate, I found I had more physical and spiritual strength—strength that I could then offer to Roger. In turn, this strength deepened my belief that no matter what happened, things would be OK. By "OK" I do not mean that things would work out exactly the way I wanted them to, but rather that no matter what happened, I could handle it.

Part of the compassion and self-compassion process includes a reminder to ourselves that we have what it takes to get through whatever we are facing.

On an airplane, in the event of an emergency, we are told to put our oxygen masks on first, prior to helping our loved ones. Instead of thinking that Roger and I shared the same mask as we journeyed through his cancer together, I came to learn the importance of acknowledging that we were still two people and we had two masks. My figurative mask had to go on first in order for me to help him with his. One of the most effective ways to put my mask on first was to do things like drink water, get some fresh air, eat healthy food, or simply *eat*! So many times, I would go all day at the hospital and forget to have even a small bite of food. Roger would have to remind me to get some sort of nourishment or hydration. One of the best things friends and family did for me on the many days I sat with Roger in the hospital was to bring me water and snacks. (Thank you, Sonia, Josibiah, Ina, Marsha, Thea, Carolyn, Don, Liza, and many others.)

University of Texas at Austin psychologist and global compassion educator Dr. Kristin Neff says that "having compassion for oneself is really no different than having compassion for others."[76] The Center for Mindful Self-Compassion teaches three elements to self-compassion:

1. Self-kindness
2. Common humanity
3. Mindfulness[77]

Neff suggests several steps to consider when offering compassion toward ourselves or others. They are as follows:

1. "Notice that they are suffering."
2. "Feel warmth, caring, and the desire to help the suffering person in some way."
3. "Realize that suffering, failure, and imperfection is part of the shared human experience."[78]

At some point, I learned to start each day with a prayer or meditation before visiting Roger in the hospital. Sometimes I would visualize myself putting on a golden shield, as if readying myself for a spiritual, moral, and health battle. I also had a "spiritual council," if you will, that I would call upon. At my "spiritual roundtable," I would visualize spiritual leaders and compassionate historical figures. At times, my mother or Mother Mary would make an appearance. Other times, it was Eleanor Roosevelt or Florence Nightingale, whom I considered to be very compassionate. Dr. Martin Luther King Jr., Abraham Lincoln, Nelson Mandela, and Sojourner Truth also appeared to me—people I felt had been through times of great suffering and had come out on the other side. Visualizing the council would provide me with great wisdom, helping me to get my thoughts in order before I had discussions with Roger or the doctors. My imaginary council most definitely helped me to do things for myself as I supported Roger.

Sometimes, I would also think about Franklin D. Roosevelt, who, at age thirty-nine, contracted a paralytic illness thought at the time to be polio but which remained a mystery to many. It was said that in 1921, when he first fell ill and Eleanor Roosevelt couldn't bear to see her husband in such anguish, she contacted several doctors, hoping one of them would be able to find a remedy for her husband's "unknown infirmity."[79] When Roger was ill, I was inspired by her actions and asked a council of doctors to meet with me about his case and care. Several mornings, I would arrive at the hospital before the doctors began their rounds. They would join me and we would start a discussion around the question "What's the plan?" Together, we debated the answers to the absolute best of our ability, given what time, energy, and resources we had on any given day.

Working with our real-life council of doctors, alongside my visualized spiritual council, helped me navigate and alleviate some of Roger's suffering. It also helped augment my capacity for compassion and self-compassion. It showed me that all of us can form a "compassionate council," whether it is an envisioned spiritual roundtable during a meditation session or a group composed of the people in our lives. Having such a team in the face of any challenging situation is necessary to help alleviate our own suffering, as well as the suffering of others.

Learning to maintain self-compassion through the greatest challenges of our lives is a constant process.

While in the midst of caring for Roger, I would often second-guess my instincts and actions. In order not to berate myself, question my thoughts or opinions, or minimize the choices I had to make, I had to become conscious of my own needs and learn how to administer more self-care. I had to constantly remind myself that I was doing the best that I could. I needed to be compassionate toward myself mentally, physically, emotionally, and spiritually. It became clear that self-compassion was very much about the acceptance of uncertainty and the ability to move forward with whatever we are able to do given our circumstances.

One of the many ways I learned to practice compassion for myself and simultaneously help others after Roger passed was to reach out to other widows and ask how I could help them. Many widows had written to me to share their stories. I actually considered launching a TV show about it at the time. While responding to them, I would share what I had learned: one of the greatest acts of self-compassion is allowing ourselves the time to grieve and telling ourselves, *It's OK to grieve the way that you are grieving.* Grief is so personal; our acts of compassion can be as well. What became clear to me through this experience was that despite the word "self-compassion" sounding very much like something we must do alone, achieving self-compassion does not happen in a vacuum. Accepting the compassion of others fuels us to be more self-compassionate. Also, it is incredible how much helping others can rejuvenate us during our own times of struggle. We may not regain the totality of our strength, though we will definitely feel a surge of energy from the heart after having supported or cared about someone else.

Beauty in the Wake of Tragedy

WHEN PRIVATE PILOT Dimitri Neonakis left the Halifax, Nova Scotia, international airport in eastern Canada just as the sun set on April 19, 2020, he didn't expect anyone to take notice of his flight path. Twenty-four hours before, a fifty-one-year-old local dentist, Gabriel Wortman, had disguised himself as a member of the Royal Canadian Mounted Police and launched a twelve-hour killing spree across sixteen crime scenes throughout the province. Twenty-two innocent lives were lost in the largest mass shooting in Canadian history. The killer targeted people he knew in rural towns, where people typically left their doors unlocked; burned five homes to the ground; and pulled over people in his mock police cruiser, killing them at random.[80] As the local authorities continued to reveal the details of this unfathomable tragedy, the community sprang into action, supporting one another as they began even the smallest attempts at putting the pieces back together. Because all of this happened in the midst of the coronavirus pandemic and physical distancing was being strictly enforced, they were not able to come together to embrace or join in vigil to honor those lost. Instead, they had to find uniquely creative ways to showcase that what residents thought to be the heart of Nova Scotia—the care, compassion, and resilience that the province's people represented—remained strong.

On the day following the massacre, in the small Nova Scotia town of Portapique, local resident Dave Brown, who was still healing from the tragedy of losing his son five years prior, wanted to give back for all the support he had received and provide hope to the community in their present need. By posting a large, red, broken heart on a telephone pole at the top of the rural road where the shooting spree began, he initiated a symbol that was quickly echoed throughout the province. His action of condolence, and the intention behind it, engendered an outpouring of love and red hearts from across the province, as the larger community rallied together.[81]

That night, when pilot Dimitri Neonakis took off in his small private plane, it was to extend his own gesture of compassion, unity, and love. Neonakis circled his plane over Portapique and many of the other affected communities, creating a flight pattern in the shape of a giant heart. He hadn't told anyone about his plan. When he returned to the airport, the first thing the air traffic controller told him was that his flight path was beautiful.[82] Neonakis wanted to let those affected know that he was thinking of them and giving the community a hug in the only way he could amid physical distancing measures. In the weeks and months that followed, he continued to contribute his flight pattern art over the province, dedicating his flight paths to fallen victims and heroes alike.

The compassion process begins with empathy.

Even the things that we think are small make a huge difference during the most challenging times.

Compassion helps us grasp what others are facing and allows us to determine how we can best provide assistance. It begins with our feelings about the suffering of other people, which propel us to reach out and offer support. It also happens when we choose to listen deeply and take the time to ask what others need; what their greatest challenges are; or what they aspire to be, do, or experience beyond their pain. Sometimes compassion is about simply being there and being fully present for someone else.

In her book *Twelve Steps to a Compassionate Life*, Karen Armstrong notes that "in Semitic languages, the word for 'compassion' (*rahamanut* in post-biblical Hebrew and *rahman* in Arabic), is related etymologically to *rehem/RHM* ('womb')."[83] The word *compassion* also literally means "to suffer with." According to the Greater Good Science Center at UC Berkeley, "Scientists have started to map the biological basis of compassion, suggesting its deep evolutionary purpose." Their research has shown that "when we feel compassion, our heart rate slows down, we secrete the 'bonding hormone' oxytocin, and regions of the brain linked to empathy, caregiving, and feelings of pleasure light up, which often results in our wanting to approach and care for other people."[84] When we're feeling empathetic and we're relating to how someone else feels, the organic next step is to want to help alleviate the suffering of others. When we offer to help someone through an act of compassion, we want to offer it in a way that the other person can receive it without feeling ashamed or humiliated, while also feeling understood. Sometimes we rush in to help, or try to solve a problem for someone without really listening to see where the person is coming from or what the individual understands about the situation. What is the person's perspective and what does he or she need at that moment?

Nonjudgmental awareness and simple acts of kindness can foster compassion.

For me, compassion is not solely about wanting to alleviate the suffering of others (bringing them to the surface), but it's also about wanting to lift the spirits of others and helping to put them on a path that can lead them to greater joy and the fulfillment of their destinies. Compassion, and how we approach it, is critically important. We have to remember that we can't always jump in encouraging others to fly. Sometimes we need to help alleviate their current suffering so that they can then slowly learn to regrow their wings and begin to fly again, living life with greater happiness and fulfillment. It is just as compassionate to want to encourage someone as it is to want to ease their suffering. According to researchers, compassion consists of five elements:

1. Recognizing suffering
2. Understanding the universality of human suffering
3. Feeling for the person suffering
4. Tolerating uncomfortable feelings
5. Acting to alleviate suffering[85]

We don't always need similar experiences to be compassionate toward one another; we just need to lean in, listen deeply, and work to understand where someone is coming from. That's why empathy precedes compassion. In that process of acting out of compassion, we may very well open ourselves up to learning something new, something of value that will help us be even more nonjudgmental and compassionate going forward. Taking baby steps to listen to and be empathetic with others can help build compassion. So can simple acts of kindness.

The Norm of Uncertainty

WHEN AUTHORITIES were advocating for everyone to regularly and rigorously wash their hands to help prevent the spread of the COVID-19 virus at the height of the pandemic, Atlanta native Terence Lester recognized that doing so would be a struggle for the population that his organization served. Lester was the cofounder of the nonprofit Love Beyond Walls, a charity that advocates for people who are homeless. Their website opens, in large white letters, with "A movement of doers" and goes on to explain the organization's vision, which is "to provide dignity to the homeless and poor by providing a voice, visibility, shelter, community, and grooming and support services to achieve self-sufficiency." Their core values are love, diversity, support, collaboration, innovation, sacrifice, and dignity.[86] In an interview with

Good Morning America, Lester said, "As the world was talking about sanitizing and washing your hands, I knew there was an entire community of people experiencing homelessness who couldn't do any of those things."[87] He opted to offer compassion in the greatest way he knew how, by setting up portable handwashing stations for the city's homeless population. As he and his team began to refill the five- to ten-gallon handwashing stations, they were amazed by how much the stations were being used each day. New York City; Austin, Texas; and Oakland, California, soon joined the initiative, providing portable sinks for their homeless populations.

We can't tell people to pull themselves up by their own bootstraps when they don't have any boots.

Before such a major global event like the pandemic presented us with the clear need for greater connection, empathy, and compassion, it could have been easy to buy into the leadership mantra of "just do what I did and you will be like me." Leaders spouting such messages may have had educational or financial advantages or benefited from certain laws or their gender; making such antiquated conditioning unrealistic in a world where a pandemic exposed even greater divides through the economies, races, and social classes within countries. When we talk about compassion, we have to think about where the person we are attempting to relate to has started from and what realistic steps we can take or help the person take. When someone feels as though they are drowning in their thoughts or struggles, they need to be brought to the surface before they can learn how to swim freely again.

Researchers Joanna Peplak and Tina Malti, in their 2021 article "Toward Generalized Concern: The Development of Compassion and Links to Kind Orientations," state that "recently, due to increased globalization and diversification, the importance of *global compassion* (i.e., compassion that is felt toward others regardless of their status, intergroup membership, or circumstance) has been highlighted. Global compassion is theorized to be fundamental in the development of a universal prosocial orientation and may motivate kindness that extends beyond one's own group." Their research concludes that "in turbulent times characterized by conflict, divide, and global crises (e.g., the COVID-19 pandemic), expanding our range of concern for others to extend across intergroup boundaries may be important for motivating reparation, cooperation, and harmony. Nurturing compassion may be particularly necessary to conquer conflict and hardship."[88]

In twelve-step groups such as Alcoholics Anonymous (AA), compassion is often learned and practiced. If someone in a meeting has had a relapse or is struggling to stop an addiction and they really want to get sober, there is no time for judgment. The group leans in and finds a way to support that person in overcoming his or her current challenges, to continue progressing forward to sobriety. And once that person is sober and grateful for being sober, their compassion for other people becomes enhanced, allowing them to pay it forward. Those in attendance are there because they are seeking support and compassion. While everyone there has lived through similar experiences, their life paths have all been different. For that reason, every participating member learns to be nonjudgmental, which plays a major role in showing compassion. Groups often work to move the dialogue beyond small talk and help members be more willing to speak openly and honestly with someone about the things that are important in life. Because Roger and I both had some experience with AA, we fell right into a compassionate dialogue from the day we met. It was one that grew into a lifelong conversation.

Positive psychology writer and educator Anna Lucas says that "in a world that is more virtually connected than ever before, social connection is waning at an alarming rate. Extensive research has demonstrated the importance of individuals' connection to others, and community, as central for holistic well-being." In her 2019 paper, "Cultivating Connection: A Conceptual Model Identifying Facilitating and Inhibiting Factors across Three Levels of Community," she introduces a recipe for authentic human connection (AHC). Authentic human connection, she says, "shows up at three levels of community: micro-communities of dyads and families, meso-communities of workplaces and schools, and macro-communities of neighborhoods, cities, and countries." The factors that can limit or inhibit AHC include "unconscious bias, fear, social and cultural norms, power structures, competition, instability, inequality, mistrust, and physical environment."[89]

Lucas presents three strategies for creating greater connection:

1. **"Cultivate compassion within ourselves and for others in our lives."** Authentic human connection," she says, "is deeply rooted in the recognition of humans' deep interdependence and connection with each other, and the environments they live. Building compassion, an other-oriented emotion, strengthens the brain's 'empathy network.' . . . Two tools that can assist with cultivating compassion within ourselves and the people around us are the practices of self-compassion and loving kindness meditation."
2. **"Give presence."** This is not about "how we show up, but that we show up, and in

person," she says. "In the 21st century with remote working options, video calls, and social media, in-person moments and interactions seem to be the exception, rather than the rule."

In times of forced social isolation, such as occurred during the COVID-19 pandemic, we need to be creative about creating "in-person moments" virtually or from a distance.

3. **"Recognize strengths."** As Lucas explains, "Character strengths and virtues are individuals' way of being and acting in the world. They are most powerful when we are aware of them, explore them, and apply them within our lives."[90]

Great challenge can help open our eyes to opportunities for compassion.

During the COVID-19 pandemic, we found ourselves in the midst of a "great pause," as some of us have called our time in quarantine. This pause led to our paying increased attention to what was happening in our communities and within ourselves. We were given the opportunity to focus on listening to the things that occurred in the lives of others and share in their lived experiences. Our eyes were opened to clearly seeing certain social situations for the first time, and for some people, this granted them a perspective inspired by newfound empathy and the desire to step up our acts of compassion and kindness. On the flip side, the repercussions of the pandemic also caused fear and anxiety, leading to a growing need for care. It was a time like never before, showing us that we all truly had to be "in this together."

There will always be uncertainty in our lives. We will not always know what is coming from a health perspective, an economic one, or a political one. Therefore, we have to be compassionate toward ourselves and others to be able to put one foot in front of the other and do whatever the next thing is to get through those times. We may not always know what the next "right" thing or "best" thing to do is, but when we act out of compassion, we will be able to find the strength to recognize that next step and take it, thereby moving ourselves forward in a constructive way.

Stretching Ourselves

IT FELT FATED that I had just arrived home and turned on the television. I don't normally watch football (unless the Chicago Bears have made the Super Bowl), though something had me sit and watch. The first quarter of Monday Night Football on January 2, 2023, had just gotten underway, featuring the Buffalo Bills and the Cincinnati Bengals. Within minutes of sitting down, I witnessed Bills safety Damar Hamlin tackle Bengals wide receiver Tee Higgins, briefly get up, then collapse back down on the turf. The Bills medical team rushed onto the field and, as we later learned, provided the lifesaving CPR hailed as what kept Damar alive after he suffered cardiac arrest. His heart had stopped beating. To the amazement of all, there was no "game must go on" rally cry that is so typical in sports. Instead, everyone came together to pray for Damar and the game was officially postponed.

That evening, there was a phenomenon of collective compassion coming together. Despite the Bills game and Damar Hamlin's circumstances playing out in an opponent's town, Cincinnati fans made their way to the UC Medical Center, where Hamlin had been rushed for treatment. From a respectful distance, they offered prayers and support. Fans in Bills jerseys and Bengals jerseys stood as one, collectively hoping for Damar's recovery. As the night rolled on, more fans gathered, and the city of Cincinnati showed its support, even lighting the downtown skyline blue. Fans bonded together and began generously donating to a toy drive Damar had been running. Donations reached $3 million by morning.[91] Four weeks after he suffered cardiac arrest on the field, Damar spoke publicly for the first time, via video. He thanked the city of Cincinnati, the Bengals, and the entire NFL for "putting team allegiance aside to root for one kid's life" and went on to say that he was not surprised by it, but deeply grateful that they had "put humanity above team loyalty, you showed the world unity over division."

He ended the video tribute by holding his hands in the form a heart.[92]

At the NFL Honors awards in February 2023, Damar Hamlin stood among the first responders who helped save his life. In his speech, he said, "Sudden cardiac arrest is something I never would have chosen to be a part of my story, but that's because our own visions are too small." His original vision was about playing in the NFL and being the best player he could be. "God's plan," he said, "was to have a purpose greater than any game in this world." He spoke about being amazed every day at how his personal experience has inspired people to spread love and to keep fighting in any circumstance. What he had been through had given others hope.[93] He is a competitor, though his story shows us that anyone can have the drive to win while also displaying compassion for the human condition. There was an innate human decency to the communal reaction that we all had to his circumstances. It was one that was felt so deeply by so many and even rippled throughout the world. The overwhelming support, love, and prayers made me feel as though I were watching miracles unfold.

When we come together in the name of collective compassion, we have the power to move mountains.

The principle of compassion has always been at the forefront of my life. I felt that I had so much to give to other people because I'd had such a loving childhood. My mother embodied compassion. There were nine of us children growing up: five girls and four boys. The energy and attention in our household always felt very balanced, between what we received from our mother and our father. Dad was more grounded in reality and provided a stable home and environment that we appreciated, yet to me, my mother was the one who always seemed to elicit a special feeling of joy. Her eyes made me feel as though she could clearly see and feel everything others were experiencing, and her world always seemed so magical and full of love. To her, compassion meant not only wanting to help alleviate others' suffering, but she also wanted to help bring light, joy, and laughter to one's life.

All the older people in the neighborhood absolutely loved my mother because she would visit them, especially if they didn't have family nearby. She would invite them to our house for tea and regularly check in to see if they needed anything. When people were sick, she would make them one of her herbal tinctures from her plants in the garden in our backyard. She would also visit the blind man down the street and make sure things were clean in his house, even though he couldn't see! She would walk him to the store where he shopped because he wanted to feel independent. Workers from the Lighthouse for the Blind taught me to read basic braille so that I could help him alongside my mother. Our home was a hub of activity in the neighborhood, for the old and young alike. Local kids would come over to play because my mother always gave them a hug, a cookie, or a kind word. My friends said that "Miss Johnnie Mae," as they called my mother, made them feel special.

Compassion enables us to do something for someone else that we may not have thought we were capable of doing.

The act of offering compassion brings a tide of positive ripple effects. In *Compassion: Concepts, Research and Applications*, Barbara L. Fredrickson writes about "a different view of love . . . as being represented by micro-moments of what I call 'positivity resonance.'" She explains, "These are collaborative, or joint experiences that unfold between two or more people. . . . These are moments in which one person's positive emotion inspires and amplifies another person's positive emotion, which in turn inspires and amplifies the first person's positive emotion." When examining these exchanges from an affective science perspective, she notes that "there are three key elements that form a temporal braid that unfolds between people." The first is a "*shared positive affective experience*," one in which an "authentic emotional positivity emerges within each person that, when expressed through smiles, nonverbal behavior, or in words, also triggers the other person's authentic positive emotions." The second is "*mutual care or concern*: a mutual orientation to be invested in the well-being of the other." And the third is "*biobehaviorial synchrony*," which occurs through a "synchrony in their facial expressions, their postures, or nonverbal communications."[94]

To me, every time my mother walked into a room, it was as though she brought the sunshine with her. Growing up, I used to think she had a special relationship with the sun. When she would lie in bed reading the Sunday paper with my dad, we would sneak into their bedroom just to see how its rays seemed to cast only upon her. It looked as if they were coming straight through the window and finding her eyes. We never understood just how that happened, though it was proof to our childhood minds that she was indeed magical. Looking back on my childhood, I think I now understand why my brothers and sisters, and even our friends and neighbors, seemed to become nicer after a visit with Mother. Could it have been that her empathy and loving compassion were helping us to secrete oxytocin, lighting up our brains' pleasure centers and resulting in our wanting to approach and care for others? I remember how my siblings pushed and shoved to get the closest seat to Mother, and how after she assured us each in turn with a hug, we sometimes willingly gave up the coveted seat.

Compassion binds us and allows us to become aware that we are not alone. It is reassuring to know that we don't have to bear the suffering by ourselves, in a vacuum. Knowing that others can feel our pain and hurt, that they are there to help us and sincerely want to help, leads to our feeling better, safer, and more secure. Reaching out to people who are hurting stretches us, enlarges us, and helps us to experience personal growth. It feels good not only to get help from others, but it feels good to help others. In this way, compassion becomes a reciprocal loop promoting a closer society.

At the 2023 ESPY Awards, Damar Hamlin tearfully presented the Buffalo Bills training staff with the Pat Tillman Award for Service. It was an emotional moment, as mirrored in the faces of those onstage as well as those in the audience. He had been given the OK by his doctors to play football again. It was abundantly clear how the outpouring of compassion and humanity that his cardiac arrest elicited had become a lesson that warmed many hearts. Damar Hamlin said the compassion and humanity he experienced had even made him a better person. Personally, it gives me hope for a better world.

Degree of Humanity

IN 1997, ARLENE SAMEN, a nurse practitioner with more than fifteen years of experience in high-risk obstetrics at University of Utah Health and years of experience at other institutions including the Navajo Nation, shared an encounter with His Holiness the Dalai Lama. At that time, it was said that one in ten Tibetan newborns and one in one hundred Tibetan pregnant women were dying during childbirth. In Tibet there was no history of training midwives to deliver babies. Women would give birth alone in animal sheds, with many losing their lives in the process.[95] His Holiness's own mother had seen only seven of her sixteen children survive to adulthood. Arlene told me that when the Dalai Lama asked for her help, she closed her clinical practice in the United States and founded

One H.E.A.R.T. (Health Education and Research in Tibet), a nonprofit organization dedicated to creating maternal and neonatal health programs in the most remote places of the world.

When they began their work, Arlene and her team joined forces with the local communities they would serve, to help understand the struggles pregnant women and newborns faced. This included learning about local traditions as well as religious and cultural beliefs so they could offer compassionate care that is culturally sensitive, comprehensive, and collaborative. Her objective was clear: to reduce the risk of maternal and infant mortality. The company's vision became to create "a locally-led health system providing equitable access to quality care for all mothers and newborns."[96] Through our frequent telephone and email conversations, Arlene shared with me the same sentiments she widely expressed. "I am so happy that One Heart has reached over a million mothers and newborns and reduced maternal mortality some years to zero," she proudly told me. "We were the first organization to train midwives, build birthing centers, and we developed our model now known as the Network of Safety. To go back, year after year, and see the families in which we saved lives . . . made me realize how connected we all are and that one drop of water makes the sea. One Heart Worldwide has been able to drive systemic behavioral change so that women no longer faced death in order to give life."[97]

Compassion is the outward display of who we truly are as humanity.

Compassion is no longer "too mushy" a topic to speak about or "too soft" a character trait to have. In today's day and age, being a compassionate person helps many of us thrive. The compassionate person is the one about whom others speak in such endearing terms, because of the impact they have had on their hearts and lives. I'm a firm believer that we were all put on this earth with some mission. Being compassionate makes us feel good. It can also serve to awaken the leader within us when we embrace the opportunity to step up and support.

The last big party I attended before the coronavirus pandemic shut everything down in 2020 was a sixtieth birthday party for my friend Chas Edelstein. Chas is an investment banker who has held several prominent positions at the heads of financial organizations and served on the boards of other organizations. When it came time for guests to get up onstage and talk about him, they easily could have referred to him as being "the money man," but almost no one spoke about what he did for a living. Nor did they speak about how much money he'd made for himself or for them, or how successful he was at his job. Instead, his broad cross section of friends, who included beloved zookeeper Jack Hanna, money guru Suze Orman, and country music singer Neal McCoy as well as politicians, childhood friends, and movie stars such as Bo Derek and Rob Schneider, spoke instead about his dedication, his care, his ability to listen, and his willingness to focus on their needs. They spoke about the trusting connection and the bond of warmth they felt with him. They gave examples of how he was quick to laugh and smile and how he could look at any dire situation and find the silver lining. They spoke about his philanthropy and his willingness to pitch in to lend a hand. Everything they shared centered around his compassionate nature—his ability to lean in, listen, and act from that place of deeply understanding those he befriended. Their words painted a picture of a man who sincerely cared about people and who helped to make their lives better through his compassionate friendship.

Compassion is a capacity we all have and one that we all can build upon.

Forgiveness opens the door and creates space for us to be more empathetic, compassionate, and kind. Empathy allows us to deeply understand and relate to others. Compassion leads us to want to help alleviate the suffering and lift the spirits of others, so they can fulfill their destinies. The next step, kindness, becomes about the simple acts that spur forgiveness, empathy, and compassion into action. On the following pages you will find questions to help you consider the ways in which you can be more compassionate toward the people in your life today and those you encounter in the future. You will also find questions designed to help you build greater self-compassion. Sit with and meditate upon them, as you offer yourself the same care that you extend to others who are suffering and in need of help raising their spirits.

Compassion Journal

Compassion Exercise 1: Stretching Ourselves

What people or community in your life have you felt true empathy toward? What individual or group do you find yourself wanting to support on a deeper level? In the following space, challenge yourself to think of ways you can transform this instinct into true compassionate action!

The person, group, or community that moves me to want to help them is . . . ______________________

____

____

____

____

____

____

____

I am drawn to help ease their suffering and lift them up so they can rise to their destinies because . . .

The concrete compassionate actions I can take to help are . . .

Compassion Exercise 2: Practicing Self-Compassion

Think about the last situation in which you exerted a great deal of physical, emotional, and/or mental energy to support someone else during a time of need, then complete the following statements.

To help alleviate the suffering of that person, I . . .

____

____

____

____

____

____

I can offer that same level of care and compassion to myself by . . . ______________________

____

____

____

____

____

____

____

____

When I do these things for myself, it will allow me to . . .

FECK PRINCIPLE 4

Kindness

Giving Changes Us

DURING CHICAGO'S POLAR vortex in January 2019, temperatures plunged to a frigid minus twenty-three degrees Fahrenheit. On the morning of January 30, local resident and businesswoman Candice Payne called her assistants, telling them not to come to work. It was too dangerously cold to commute. Her intention had been to have a regular workday at home . . . until she began thinking about those who lived outside, without a home in which to escape the cold. Within a matter of hours, Candice had used her personal credit card to secure twenty hotel rooms at the Amber Inn motel—the only place willing to take in the homeless. She then took to social media, sharing about her mission and asking for anyone with a truck or van to help transport the homeless to the hotel rooms. Her post went viral.[98] What began as a gesture of incredible kindness to house people for a single night turned into securing seventy-two rooms over five nights, helping 122 people get in from the cold. Pregnant women, children, disabled people, those who had just been released from the hospital after surgery—all had a place to stay.

In her February 2019 interview on *The Ellen DeGeneres Show*, Candice shared that her boyfriend had once been homeless. She spoke about wanting to break the misconception that certain people are lazy or don't want to work. She addressed the reality that so many people are just one paycheck away from becoming homeless.[99] When Candice had previously started a nonprofit called Action for a Cause, she didn't know what she wanted to do with the charity. Today her mission is abundantly clear: she uses her passion for real estate to help house people by rehabilitating distressed multiunit buildings.[100] It is her hope that others will jump on the bandwagon with her and support the cause.

Kindness is an active uplifting of those around us.

Mahatma Gandhi reportedly said, "It's the action, not the fruit of the action, that's important. You have to do the right thing. It may not be in your power, may not be in your time, that there will be any fruit. But that doesn't mean you stop doing the right thing. You may never know what results come from your action. But if you do nothing, there will be no result."[101] This is why we give of ourselves through acts of kindness.

Researchers Peplak and Malti define having a "kind orientation" as "one's propensity to experience emotions, thoughts, and express behaviors that reflect fairness, care, and a concern for the welfare of others."[102] To me, kindness is about the acts we perform to help uplift others in their lives, careers, and interactions with others. These acts can benefit greatly from our creativity and our ability to step outside of our comfort zones to make unsolicited contributions, big or small, to others or to our communities. Care, love, and concern also fuel kindness as equally as they do forgiveness, empathy, and compassion.

In a 2018 article titled "Happy to Help? A Systematic Review and Meta-Analysis of the Effects of Performing Acts of Kindness on the Well-Being of the Actor," researchers defined kindness as "actions intended to benefit others." They also explored various forms of kindness, including the following:

1. Kin altruism: kindness to our families
2. Mutualism: kindness to members of our communities
3. Reciprocal altruism: kindness to those we know we may encounter again
4. Competitive altruism: kindness to others in order to enhance our status (not the type of kindness we are talking about in this book)[103]

When I was growing up, I would sometimes become flooded with overwhelming feelings about the goodness in the world. In turn, these feelings made me want to go out and do good things for others. I was also the recipient of immense kindness from my mother, father, and siblings. While I know it may sound naive now, my heart often felt as if it would explode because people were so good. My mother was the only one who treated those feelings as normal. She called them "moments of grace" and believed that sometimes God or the universe just shows us what is possible . . . and if we are lucky, that grace bubbles up inside of us enough that we find a way of sharing it with the world.

My childhood gifted me with the security of feeling that I have kindness and love within me and surrounding me. It has always felt natural to want to share that feeling so others may feel it too. Today, when I have those feelings of grace, I sometimes envision a cadre of people across the globe, of diverse genders, ethnicities, sizes, ages, religions, and physical abilities, riding the wave of grace with me. Feeling, if only for a moment, a sense of such glorious wholeness, health, happiness, and magnanimity toward our fellow beings.

Truly feeling another person's situation can help bring about acts of kindness, because we want to help alleviate suffering and be more compassionate.

I am not naive enough to believe that there is one panacea to the struggles we are facing individually and as a society. Though, just as producer Shonda Rhimes chose to see "diversity" as "normalizing," I'd like to see kindness normalized. What we contribute can make a difference. It is a special thing when we witness an act of kindness so selfless and touching that it makes us want to either cry or go out and do something kind for someone else. I love the way Roger used to put it: "I believe that if, at the end of it all, according to our abilities, we have done something to make others a little happier, and something to make ourselves a little happier, that is about the best we can do."

Nurturing the Child Within

CBS JOURNALIST STEVE HARTMAN reports regularly on goodness and kindness. I first noticed his "Kindness 101" segment on *CBS Mornings* with Gayle King, Tony Dokoupil, and Nate Burleson, when Steve enlisted the help of his son and daughter to illustrate how we can be kind in our everyday lives. Together they used a dictionary to define the word "kindness," then they found examples of kind acts we could perform to give the word "kindness" a real-world application. But it was one of Hartman's weekly "On the Road" segments that truly captured my attention, tugging at my heartstrings, especially because of all the people who had been left in need as a result of the pandemic, climate change, refugee crises, and economic difficulties.

On June 9, 2023, Steve cast a light on a deeply

moving story about Roderick Duncan, the owner of GodBody 901 gym in Memphis, Tennessee. Roderick had found twenty-four-year-old Brian Taylor asleep in one of the old cars he had left parked behind his gym. Knocking on the window of the car, he ordered Brian out of the vehicle. The next morning when he went to open the gym, Brian was asleep in the car again. Roderick demanded Brian get out once more, and the cycle continued. Several days later, when Roderick arrived to open the gym and found Brian asleep in his car, he chose not to alert the police; instead, he leaned in and tried a different tack. Before he tapped on the window to awaken Brian, he made him a cup of instant coffee. It was an act of kindness that surprised the young man and led to a conversation in which he opened up to Roderick about his troubled childhood and drinking problem.

In addition to helping Brian get clean clothes and transportation to attend job interviews, Roderick encouraged Brian to make other attempts at living a more normal life. Brian wasn't always perfect. When he didn't live up to what he said he would do, Roderick threatened to stop helping him. But then he'd reconsider, reasoning, "Some people need more than one chance. It takes a while for most kids to stop bumping their head." Brian credits his commitment to changing and becoming a better person to Roderick's acts of kindness and his efforts to establish a friendship with him. It was a story that could have ended very differently. We may never know why Roderick Duncan decided to give Brian Taylor a cup of coffee instead of calling the police. But the life-altering connections made between these two young men can only make the world a better place. "Real change never happens overnight," said Roderick, "but it always starts in an instant" . . . or with a cup of instant coffee.[104]

While our model for relating to another human being is heavily influenced by what we have known growing up, how we do it is ultimately our choice.

I have an extended-family member who said that the acts of kindness shown to her by our family taught her something she didn't know was possible—that someone can be kind for no reason at all. She grew up going from foster home to foster home where acts of kindness were in short supply. It was her experience that when people were kind to you, they wanted something in return. She became wary and lost trust in many people, including her own family members. Her healing began when she came to understand that it is possible to be kind to someone without expecting anything in return. Once she began to trust that she could accept an act of kindness without any quid pro quo, it made her want to do something kind for someone else—not because she had to, but because she truly wanted to. As she began to practice kindness without strings attached, it was important to her to let the receiving person know that she wanted nothing in return. That kind of giving remained a radical thought for her. After having been frequently told that everybody came from a dysfunctional family, it was the most beautiful thing when she learned there are families and countless people who are nurturing and loving.

Her relationship with kindness had forever changed.

Why embrace kindness? Number one, we have to nurture the child within each of us, especially if that child was not nurtured, loved, and made to feel secure when young. Child abuse is damaging. And I get just as torn up about gross neglect, which leaves a child feeling unwanted, unloved, and damaged too. All children deserve to be cared for and given the opportunity to be so loved that they learn to develop a true, trusted, loving connection to other human beings. It is fundamentally important to feel that kind of care and love at a young age. Even if one has grown older, it is imperative after facing circumstances where care wasn't present that at least one person intervenes to offer help and hope with acts of kindness or love so that the child within can begin to heal.

A three-year applied research initiative in Comuna 13, "a Colombian community with high levels of civil conflict," involved implementing strengthened municipal child-protection systems with the objective of improving hope and outcomes for children. This work included building capacity for caregiver empathy by combining a positive parenting approach with community early-learning strengths, child rights, and community empowerment methods. They also created "'pathways for peace,' or zones of peace in violent neighborhoods." The initiative showed that an "integrated empathy and empowerment approach resulted in improved outcomes for children and their families."[105]

We cannot underestimate the importance of kindness today and every day for our youth and to nurture the child within each of us.

When we're not the recipients of enough kindness, it affects us, personally and globally. When researchers Peplak and Malti studied a group of youth ages seven to fifteen, it was to determine how they experienced both personal and global compassion and how this factored into the development of kindness. They wanted to explore children's narratives at the time they felt compassion, because, as they state, "compassion underlies kindness and as such, is important for creating harmonious societies."[106] I agree wholeheartedly.

Healing the child within us is critically important. There is a saying that goes "Hurt people hurt people." Because I grew up surrounded by love, compassion, and kindness, I was surprised to learn about the number of people who say they have experienced some sort of childhood trauma that left them feeling unloved, unprotected, and unworthy. Instead of receiving acts of kindness, far too many children experience a very different reality. They grow up yearning for some demonstration from others that they matter and are loved. One remedy for helping to heal childhood trauma is to offer and be the recipient of acts of kindness. We can heal the child within each of us when we do this with intention. Awareness has helped us to make progress, though there remains much work to be done. Each of us plays a role in offering kindness to one another every day, and in teaching our children to do the same.

When Great Ideas Come to Life

WHEN ASPIRING FILMMAKER and Ebert Fellow Jason Yue first met Alec Eickert, Alec had a dream that had been in the works since his father passed away. In honor of his dad, Alec vowed to climb the highest points in all fifty US states to celebrate his father's life. Without hesitation, Jason agreed to also take on the adventure, which was one of several on his own personal bucket list. Together, Jason and Alec co-created the 50 States, 50 Summits project and set out to climb peaks across the country. Neither one of them had any camping or climbing experience. Their intention was to get closer to the natural world. At each stop of their journey, they immersed themselves in the great outdoors and ended up not wanting to leave. After completing a trek, they would return to their home base in the city only to have the woods call them back. There was something about being in the wilderness that began to change the way they thought about living in an economy that demands our constant attention.

With the awakenings of nature as their catalyst, the two young men sought answers to such questions as "How do we love?" Their story quickly evolved into one about humanity and the kind, caring people they met along the way. Jason told me what they learned was that most people are good and that this goodness permeates across every superficial distinction we may use to divide ourselves. He told me that he undertook this journey to find his purpose in life, gain a better understanding of others, and get closer to those whose opinions were the opposite of his own. Jason and Alec's mission had quickly become one of actionably sharing messages about what can be discovered when we escape the status quo and get out of our comfort zones, just as they had done.

What Jason Yue wants to achieve in this world is the very definition of goodness. He has chosen to apply his skills as a filmmaker to undertake an incredible act of friendship and kindness, because, as he told me, "I don't have huge dreams, but my sweet spot in life is helping execute on great ideas that I really believe in." Since Jason and Alec met, they've spent two years climbing heights in forty-one states, while putting together the foundation for a feature documentary along the way. As I write this book, I am eagerly awaiting the result of Jason's film about empathy and kindness. Already, I can feel the happiness endorphins forming in my body just knowing that Jason took to heart the emphasis on the FECK principles we addressed when he went through one of our fellowship programs. As he was filming and appreciating the country's natural beauty, he would contact me to tell me that the principles of forgiveness, empathy, compassion, and kindness had changed his outlook on life. Our conversations left me in tears. To me, Jason is an ambassador of compassion and has already expanded his impact by using his background as an engineering graduate to build a technology platform that helps encourage empathy and kindness. I can't wait to try it out.

Kindness helps bring us closer together as individuals who form our one collective human race.

In addition to nurturing the child within all of us, the second reason kindness is critical is because we feel better when we are being kind toward another person. Such acts help to change others for the better, but they also help to change us. Empathizing with another person's situation helps to bring about an act of kindness. In 2018, Yale psychology professor Laurie Santos launched a course on the science of happiness that attracted major media coverage and more student enrollment than any other course in the university's three-hundred-plus-year history. That same course, now titled "The Science of Well-Being," went viral, attracting 1.5 million students during a four-week period amid the COVID-19 pandemic and another 1.5 million in the months that followed. The course curriculum required that participants "track their sleep patterns, keep a gratitude journal, perform random acts of kindness, and take note of whether, over time, these behaviors correlate with a positive change in their general mood." Students who were asked about the results of taking the class noted effects such as greater gratitude, becoming more introspective, and feeling longer-lasting happiness.[107] When asked in an interview about the "secret to happiness," Santos said, "We think happiness is all about self care and being selfish, and kind of treating yourself, but actually happy people tend to be more focused on others. They do random acts of kindness, they give more to charities, they volunteer more of their time."[108]

Seventeenth-century clergyman and English poet John Donne stated, in his "No man is an island" poem, that *"no man is an island, entire of itself; every man is a piece of the continent, a part of the main. If a clod be washed away by the sea, Europe is the less, as well as if a promontory were, as well as if a manor of thy friend's or of thine own were. Any man's death diminishes me, because I am involved in mankind; and therefore never send to know for whom the bell tolls; it tolls for thee."*[109] I truly believe that we cannot go it alone, and that we are not meant to do anything in isolation. This applies to us as humanity, as all races, countries, and species.

Mia, the teenaged daughter of friends of mine from California, reminded me to emphasize the importance of extending kindness to animals as well. It is Mia's belief that cats, dogs, and all animals need us as much as we need them. Every Saturday since she was ten years old, she has volunteered at the Muttville Senior Dog Rescue charitable organization in San Francisco. In her time working there, she has helped people through the technical side of the animal adoption process and also started a Muttville club at her high school, where the group worked together to fundraise and spread the word about the Muttville organization. Her proudest accomplishment was establishing a "Junior Cuddle Club" in partnership with the San Francisco Mission chapter of the Boys & Girls Club. The program helps bring Muttville's dogs over the age of seven to children for cuddles. Mia says that her experience has truly demonstrated the healing power that animals can have. When I asked her what kept her so dedicated to this cause, she said it made her happy to know that the animals were getting the love and care they needed. In her words, "I don't volunteer at Muttville because of senior dogs' tragic backstories. When I'm there, I'm part of a magical place where missing lower jaws become toothy grins and arthritic waddles transform into lively dances. At every Saturday adoption event, I see people become entranced by Glen Coco's limbless hops and Nutter Butter's eyeless winks. I see petless families return every weekend to meet overweight chihuahuas and toothless dachshunds, as they come to learn these senior dogs are angels with tails." Mia's mom and dad, Rachel and Ty, are so proud of her. To say that her inner goodness shines through in this work and beyond would be an understatement. As Mia prepares to graduate and head to Stanford, I can't wait to see what type of goodness she continues to create in the world.

Kindness is a required ingredient of our humanity because it is a thread of human connection. When I see examples of others, including young people like Mia, having such feelings of grace and care for humanity, I can clearly envision the kinder, gentler world they are engendering. It is my hope that every one of us can feel, if only for a minute, the abundantly glorious love they are extending toward our fellow beings, whether human or furry and four-legged.

Reciprocal Kindness

IN 1951, WHEN JAMES HARRISON was fourteen years old, he required major chest surgery. Were it not for the thirteen units of blood he received from strangers' donations, he would not have lived. After recovering, he went on to do more than simply survive. When he learned of the kindness of the strangers who had so generously given the blood that helped save his life, he made a pledge to also donate as soon as he reached the legal donating age of eighteen. Now, at age eighty-six, James can proudly say he has donated blood more than 1,100 times over the course of sixty years. The "Man with the Golden Arm," as he became known, gave his last donation on May 11, 2018. He was eighty-one at the time, the oldest age one is qualified to be a donor. That is not where his story ends, however.

The legacy of his donations lives on within the next generation. Ten years after James began donating, it was discovered that his blood plasma contained a unique disease-fighting antibody used to develop a lifesaving injection called anti-D. In 1966, scientists at the International Society of Blood Transfusion Congress in Sydney, Australia, announced that an injection of anti-D provides enough antibodies to reduce the risk of hemolytic disease of the newborn (HDN), which occurs when a mother's blood cells attack her unborn baby's blood cells. This happens when an Rh-negative mother has a baby with an Rh-positive father. Without anti-D, at-risk babies can suffer severe liver, spleen, and brain damage, or even death. It was an announcement that was met with speculation, even by the American National Institutes of Health. Upon realizing that his blood type contained the lifesaving antibodies, James made the switch to donating plasma and became a pioneer in the Australian Red Cross's anti-D program.[110]

Since 1967, more than three million doses of anti-D have been given to Australian mothers at risk of HDN, and James has been credited with helping to save 2.5 million babies.[111] This astonishing number caught me off guard and made me weep at this stunning example of goodness and the incredible impact James's kindness has had. His reciprocity in donating blood in return for the donations that had saved his life went above and beyond. What's more is that, according to the Australian Red Cross Blood Donor Service, every dose of anti-D ever produced in Australia has been derived from James's blood! The only place for mothers to get the anti-D antibodies is from plasma donations—and more specifically, plasma donations from those who have, at some point, become sensitized to the antigens. They are the only ones who have the crucial anti-D antibody. For James, it is medically predicted that the thirteen units of blood transfusions he received at fourteen could very well have contained the antigens, which James had by the "bucketload." Very few people have the antibodies in such strong concentrations, and every time James would donate, his body produced even more.[112]

Over the years, the number of HDN cases has gone from being as common as one in seven pregnancies to now being considered "incredibly rare."[113] In 1999, for his record-breaking number of lifesaving donations, James was awarded the Medal of the Order of Australia, one of the country's most prestigious honors. His message to the Australian community was simple: "I hope it's a record that somebody breaks, because it will mean they are dedicated to the cause."[114]

The greatest importance of kindness may be evidenced in the reciprocity theory—the principle of wanting to offer to others the same kindness offered to us.[115]

Just as hurt people hurt people, those who engage in acts of kindness generate more acts of kindness. In their 2016 *Harvard Business Review* paper, "The Trickle-Down Effect of Good (and Bad) Leadership," researchers Jack Zenger and Joseph Folkman state, "We know that emotions are contagious. Research by UC San Diego's James Fowler and Harvard's Nicholas Christakis has shown that happiness is contagious, for example. If you have a friend who is happy, the probability that you will be happier rises by 25%. We also know that behaviors are contagious. Christakis and Fowler determined that if you have overweight friends, you're more likely to be overweight yourself. If you quit smoking, your friends are more likely to quit."[116] This is to say that everything we do for good (or for bad) has a "trickle-down effect."

Many are familiar with the momentum of the pay-it-forward philosophy, said to be popularized by Benjamin Franklin in 1784. "In a pay-it-forward system, a person receives a gift . . ." such as an act of kindness "and then is provided the opportunity to give a gift to another. It is an example of upstream reciprocity theory," whereby the recipient of the gift of kindness feels a "'warm glow' that makes them more likely to help other, unspecified people."[117] The theory of reciprocity, which has become more popular in recent years, is based "on the assumption that people are willing to reward kind acts and to punish unkind ones."[118]

Kindness changes not only the person to whom it is shown, but it also changes the person performing the kindness. We get a two-for-one exchange of humanity that provides benefits all around. I have found that when I perform an act of care or concern for another's well-being, it actually makes me feel happier. Fascinatingly, science supports "that being kind (i.e., a prosocial behavior) was associated with well-being." From an organizational standpoint, upstream reciprocity can potentially lead to "improved teamwork, enhanced creativity and stronger engagement."[119] It is also said that after we receive help from others, "there is a perceived social obligation to help another person who needs it." All aspects of paying it forward or reciprocity theory are said to "increase community solidarity and decrease some of the financial barriers" of caring for people in need.[120]

I believe that the story of eighty-six-year-old James Harrison's kindness is one of the greatest examples to illustrate the reciprocity theory principle. While some perform acts of kindness simply because they desire to be kind, others may do so in return for kindness that has been offered to them. It's important to note, however, that the dynamics of reciprocity theory also hold true for receiving acts of unkindness and for being unkind toward others, thereby making the need to foster kindness that much greater.

Never underestimate the positive impact of an act as simple as a compliment or a kind smile.

Kindness is ultimately about getting away from focusing on ourselves and getting into the spirit of giving something of ourselves. It is about leading with fun energy and doing something that has nothing to do with fulfilling our own wants. For some of us, that may mean joining a charitable organization or a group that has a specific need, such as the Boys & Girls Club; for others, it may involve extending a smile to a stranger. What matters is that we act and choose to do something that has nothing to do with ourselves or our personal benefits. What we specifically choose to contribute of our time, effort, or money is up to each of us.

The Simplest of Acts

IN 2011, ELITE AUSTRALIAN cricketer Kath Koschel made her debut for the New South Wales team. Since she was eight years old, her goal had been to play professionally. But just as her dream career was getting started, it came to a painfully abrupt halt. Kath sustained a back injury, complications of which posed the risk of having to have a leg amputated. While a second emergency surgery did lead to saving a leg, Kath faced a long rehabilitation journey. During that period, she formed an instant connection with a man named Jim. The two fell in love and began planning a future together, until tragedy struck again in 2012, when Jim took his own life. Kath felt herself returning to the same darkness she'd grappled with following her career-ending injury. The burden of physical and mental trauma was weighing heavily upon her. She had lost the man who represented the brightest shining light in that abyss, and she didn't know where to go from there.

As she worked to find a path forward, acts of kindness offered by others who simply wanted to help provided the glimmers of light that ultimately led the way. While some offered random small gestures, such as opening a door for her as she navigated her way around, others offered more personalized support. Regardless of what the acts were, one thing became clear to Kath: little things were adding up to make a really big difference. Kindness inspired her to find the strength to raise over $300,000 for various charity organizations, even as she continued to push through her own challenges. By September 2015, her perseverance led her to become the first person with prosthetic discs in her back to complete an Ironman Triathlon. In the process, she became hooked on both endurance sports and the power of kindness. [121]

On November 13, 2015, Kath Koschel founded the Kindness Factory, a nonprofit on a mission to "make the world a kinder place." Fueled by her desire to show others how powerful kindness can be, she dedicated herself to building a message and platform that could touch the world. Things were gaining momentum faster than her legs were gliding her through her triathlons, when she was suddenly hit from behind by a truck while training for her second Ironman in 2016. Left with a broken back and life-threatening injuries for a second time, the darkness that had plagued her once before began to creep back in. Yet this time was different, as kindness remained all around her. Her website and social media feeds were flooded with uplifting words from others moved by her story. In that moment, Kath's unshakable belief was tested and proven: we do indeed all have the capacity for kindness. It is this principle that she credits for saving her life.[122]

Sometimes the simplest acts of kindness become the most powerful.

In its first seven years, the Kindness Factory logged nearly five million acts of kindness. In May 2020, after joining forces with a team of academics, Kath and her collaborators at Kaplan, a leading global provider of educational programs, launched the Kindness Curriculum.[123] Within its first year and a half, the curriculum was being used by more than 3,500 schools across Australia, the US, and the UK. The message of the Kindness Curriculum is that "kindness is a preventative tactic." In the words of its creators, the curriculum "work[s] with our school partners to implement programs to address bullying, mental ill health, collaboration and cooperation, respect, resilience and more." As Kath has said, "It's not our job to toughen our children up to face a cruel and heartless world. It's our job to raise children who will make the world a little less cruel and heartless."[124] She has no plans of slowing the global spread of what kindness can do. November 13, the day the Kindness Factory was founded in 2015, has been named World Kindness Day, and Kath and the teams at the Kindness Factory and Kindness Curriculum continue to spread the message of kindness through #onesmallact at a time.

Kindness is achieved by beginning to identify ways that we can help others. Each of us gets to decide what that looks like for us.

When I talk about kindness, it encompasses many acts, big and small. Some people think it doesn't count if it isn't a monumental deed, but nothing could be further from the truth. In the 2020 article "Rewards of Kindness? A Meta-Analysis of the Link between Prosociality and Well-Being," researchers reveal just how much our less formal acts of kindness can benefit people. "Informal helping (vs. formal helping) was linked to more well-being benefits."[125] We never fully know what another person is going through. If there is even the smallest act we can do to help another person get through the day, then why not do it? Experience has helped me clearly see that kindness can be achieved through our interactions, conversations, and actions, often in the simplest ways.

For some of us, it can feel daunting to take or

even receive a deliberate act of kindness. A simple gesture or word of kindness inserted into an interaction or conversation may feel like a much easier first step. Big or small, any act of kindness is a great place to start. Although an act of kindness sometimes consists of a financial contribution, please do not equate kindness with having to spend or give money. Giving a FECK isn't about making million-dollar contributions to community centers. While those donations are nice and welcomed, this movement is ultimately about each and every one of us doing small acts that have big impacts. So many things that people do for us every day, or that we do for others, can be considered kind. It doesn't require a lot to do something for someone else, and by committing acts of kindness on a regular basis, it becomes a muscle that gets stronger and more able with use, so exercise it often. The same holds true on a global level, as from our acts of kindness come moments of grace and gratitude—something we could undoubtedly use more of in our world. The extent of the positive effect of kindness (and all the FECK principles) is truly up to each of us. If we all contribute small actions with big impacts more regularly, the results might just change the world for the better.

Watching Miracles Happen

IN THE BRIEF WINDOW of opportunity when Broadway reopened during the COVID-19 pandemic, I was privileged to spend time in New York going to the theater every night. I was looking forward to seeing *To Kill a Mockingbird*, based on the classic American novel by Harper Lee, and *Tina*, the musical about the now late, great Tina Turner. I also went to see *Come from Away*, a play I was not as familiar with and one that had flown a bit under my radar. Walking into the theater, I knew only that it had something to do with 9/11. What I soon learned was that *Come from Away* is based on a true story about Gander, Newfoundland, a town of barely eight thousand people at that time. When the terrorists flew through the Twin Towers of the World Trade Center in New York on September 11, 2001, and airspace was temporarily shut down with no planes able to enter or leave the United States, flights from overseas were diverted to the tiny town of Gander. At its peak, thirty-eight planes carrying approximately seven thousand passengers were grounded there, doubling the population of the small town and leaving its residents rushing to help and play host.[126]

After spending hours grounded on the tarmac, travelers were transported to local Salvation Army shelters, churches, schools, and community centers as the townspeople determined how they would house the immediate influx of people in need.[127] With a limited number of large hotels, local residents came together to help everyone find places to sleep and constructed makeshift accommodations for them to shower and wash their clothes. They took in complete strangers and helped entertain them, comforting the ones who were scared and lonely. They provided shelter and support for their guests for an entire week.

Bonnie Earle-Harris, head of the local Gander SPCA animal shelter, asked to see the aircrafts' manifests, because she suspected there were animals stranded in the bowels of the planes. She was right and quickly sprang into action to support nine cats, eleven dogs, and a pair of endangered apes. Because they were not able to take the animals off the planes, SPCA staff crawled into the dark cargo holds of the planes to comfort the frightened pets. On the second day, Earle-Harris and local veterinarian Dr. Doug Tweedy transformed an empty hangar into a space where all the animals could stretch and run over the next five days.[128] Gander's kindness quickly extended to all sentient beings.

I had no idea all of this had taken place! Watching that play was not only a surprise to me but a supreme revelation confirming the Goodness (with a capital *G)* of people. After the show concluded, I floated out of the theater feeling as if I were on a cloud, gobsmacked after witnessing the most complete exhibition of unconditional compassion and kindness I had ever seen on a stage. The impact of it continued to ripple within me, and it was as though I could see the wonder in the eyes of the other patrons as they made their way out of the theater, seemingly changed. As my friend Chris and I headed back out to the street, we came upon an older woman walking ahead of us. She had an obvious limp and was accompanied by a younger woman who was helping her. I watched them glance at the pedicabs lined up outside the theater. I could see the naked longing in the eye of the woman with the limp. And just to make sure I wasn't imagining this, I asked Chris. He, too, saw it and recognized the desire of the older woman for the easier means of transportation provided by the cabs. Then it happened. Someone quietly went to one of the pedicab drivers and exchanged money while pointing to the limping woman and her friend. The good citizen then caught up with the ladies and casually asked if they would prefer to ride in the pedicab, rather than walk. The ladies replied by saying that it was probably too expensive an option for them. As it turned out, it was not. The Good Samaritan told them it was their lucky night and that the pedicab driver had just announced someone was going to get a free ride! "No charge," the driver merrily called out. Both ladies happily hopped on board and waved to us all with big smiles on their faces as they were whisked away.

As we turned around, I noticed a tall, handsome man wearing a dark blue suit and a white collar standing outside of the theater. Whether his white collar denoted he was a clergyman, I do not know. He was simply standing there, watching the dispersing crowd with benevolent-looking eyes. As I walked past him, he said in almost a whisper, as if he were praying: “I like to stand here and watch the miracles happen.” *What!* I was so startled and awestruck by his words. Then he repeated it: “I like to stand here and watch the miracles happen.” He then shared that he had never seen so much good in people as he had witnessed standing outside of that theater when *Come from Away* would let out. It was one of his favorite places to be because he saw people come out changed and he had never seen that before when people were leaving a play.

I ran to catch up with Chris and asked him if he had heard what the well-dressed man had said about the miracles. “What man?” he asked, causing me to think that perhaps I was having my own personal hallucination, like the angels visiting George Bailey in *It’s a Wonderful Life*. As I debated whether this was a moment of temporary insanity, Chris confirmed that he, too, had seen the man, though he had not heard what he whispered as we passed. Regardless, it was all very real to me. *Come from Away* and an angelic man watching miracles happen caused my heart to burst wide open. It was clear that even theater, when noble, can be a catalyst for acts of love and kindness. Those were the feelings I wished for every one of our personal experiences with kindness to imbue.

We create better communities by doing the things that empower us to become our best selves.

On April 4, 2017, the fourth anniversary of what Roger called his "leave of presence" from this world (and coincidently the day of the death of the Reverend Dr. Martin Luther King Jr. in 1968), we celebrated Roger's life and legacy, but more importantly, we celebrated all the things he stood for. In an effort to continue his mission to spread messages of empathy, and to honor his life, I created #Day4Empathy. It was declared in tribute to reinforce Roger's staunch belief in the necessity of humility and compassion, and of paying forward acts of kindness. The day served as a call to action for more of us to exhibit our inherent goodness, to step up with compassion and kindness in our everyday interactions with other people, whether at work, study, or play. The idea was to help create a better community by drawing each one of us closer to being our own best selves. The celebration was designed to encourage us all to have conversations with one another and with children that impress upon them the many beautiful reasons why they should try to relate to people who are different from them. It is a day to inspire watercooler conversations about what empathy means to us, and to talk about and demonstrate how it helps make our communities and lives better. Part of the goal of #Day4Empathy was to ignite an ongoing conversation about the transformative nature of Roger's compass of values in today's divisive landscape and issue a loud and resounding call to action. It was to ignite the same kinds of acts that the man in the blue suit watched play out as the patrons of *Come from Away* exited the theater.

Looking someone in the eyes, smiling, and saying "hello" is indeed a monumental action, one we can all engage in to spread more kindness.

On the first #Day4Empathy in 2017, all those who participated handed out kindness cards and bracelets, encouraged random acts of kindness around Chicago, talked with residents, and planted that seed of empathy everywhere they could in the hopes of it taking root. One participant simply went around saying "Hello!" to everyone. I thought about his action a lot, because it was one of the simplest ways that he could show kindness. The idea of simply saying hello grew inside me, knowing how often we walk around in our own little worlds looking down at our phones or other devices. We close ourselves off from others. We don't look up to see who's walking toward or beside us. Sometimes all it takes is walking a little slower, listening a little more intently, or looking into someone's eyes to help create those moments of kindness when miracles truly do happen. As it turns out, everything I was feeling was supported in the 2023 Gallup National Health and Well-Being Index. Over 4,500 US adults were surveyed, and the conclusion was that those "who regularly say hello" to up to six people in their neighborhoods "have higher well-being than those who greet fewer or no neighbors." From greeting no neighbors to greeting up to six, the social, community, career, physical, and financial well-being scores increased steadily with each additional neighbor greeted.[129]

For me, exercising kindness and empathy in Roger's honor was an opportunity to develop the ability to look at the good in any person and to forgive indiscretions. Roger had a heightened ability to do just that. I do not mean this in a simplistic or reductive manner. He did not overlook the bad; he acknowledged it, but he somehow managed to take into account the totality of the person and what he or she contributed to society or to our lives. By amplifying the good, it allowed him to be more tolerant and forgiving. This was especially true if someone had the decency to be self-aware and remorseful and, in their own way, was trying to evolve. In my experience, when someone perceives you as your better self, it makes you want to live up to it. Each and every one of us deserves to have someone who perceives the good in us and who makes us want to be a better person. Someone who counts on us to display our better nature and give forth the kind gestures that make miracles happen. Living in alignment with the FECK principles does that.

A Goodness That Permeates

AT THE ROGER EBERT CENTER for film studies at the University of Illinois at Urbana-Champaign, in the College of Media, our purpose and mission is to inspire and educate emerging writers, artists, filmmakers, and technologists to tell stories that matter, whether in the world of cinema or with inventions in the realm of technology. The Roger Ebert Center helps them create and relay stories that bring the human race closer together instead of dividing us. It gives them firsthand experience of how films can affect and truly connect others through forgiveness, empathy, compassion, and kindness. It began when Roger and I launched the endowment for the center, based on a single initial donation in 2009. Through the kindness of donors, some of them anonymous, the Roger

Ebert Center has become a reality. The vision and hope has been that, no matter their race, gender, age, religion, or other aspects of their identity, aspiring business leaders and filmmakers take to heart the program's mission and practice the principles of forgiveness, empathy, compassion, and/or kindness in their writing, art, or technology. While waiting for the center to become fully realized, I worked with the various deans of the College of Media to establish an Ebert Symposium and a year-round Ebert Fellowship program. Roger told me that the University of Illinois had contributed so much to his life, and he wanted to find a way to give back.

In 2014, Sundance Institute founder Robert Redford launched a separate Roger Ebert Fellowship to honor and continue Roger's work regarding empathy in films at the Sundance Film Festival. The workshop brings together emerging film writers, critics, and filmmakers for mentorship and is designed as an extraordinary opportunity for them to navigate the fast-paced, deadline-driven environment of one of the world's premier film festivals. Each year (until the program was merged with the Sundance Outreach and Inclusion initiative), the Ebert Fellows who had gone through the workshop would share their stories, writing reviews and features under the tutelage of editors at RogerEbert.com. The first year, they were even mentored by Eric Kohn, a film critic from IndieWire, a media company seen perhaps as a competitor to RogerEbert.com. Similarly, the Ebert Fellows program at the University of Illinois is mentored by Michael Phillips, the film critic for the *Chicago Tribune*, the local newspaper that was seen as a competitor to Roger's newspaper, the *Chicago Sun-Times*. I mention these two men in particular because when we worked together, there was only goodness, kindness, compassion, and a fervent desire to encourage emerging film writers or film critics to be as great as they could be. I am grateful for their generosity.

The Ebert Fellows who went through these programs did so while networking with industry professionals, including directors, actors, film critics, festival programmers, agents, distributors, and publicists. The primary focus remained how to encourage and foster forgiveness, empathy, compassion, and kindness. The program gained such momentum that the Ebert Fellowship programs were temporarily extended to the Telluride Film Festival, the Chicago International Film Festival, the Columbia College Links Journalism program, the Chicago Urban League, the Hawaii International Film Festival Young Critics program, and Film Independent's Project Involve.

Through the Ebert Foundation and these various organizations and endeavors, we have supported several hundred Ebert Fellows—emerging filmmakers, film critics, and technologists—who have been given grants and mentoring. The mission behind the Ebert Fellowship has always been to put into place an incubator to develop "ambassadors of compassion" who can carry the word about the four FECK principles—not to celebrate Roger or any individual, but to see what could come of their own ideas around empathy. Their challenge was to go out into the world to awaken others to the bigger-than-life feelings that Roger felt were possible through empathy.

Our Ebert Fellows have each contributed forgiveness, empathy, compassion, or kindness in their own unique way. While writing this book, I knew I wanted to include some of their stories, because every time I think of what they are doing in the world, it warms my heart. Ebert Fellow Sue-Ellen Chitunya, for instance, travels back home to Zimbabwe with toys, books, and gently worn clothes from her own closet and those donated by friends. She gives them to an organization that houses AIDS orphans and patients, along with a start-up school for autistic children. When she sees the smiles on their faces, she is always reminded of how far a small act of kindness can go. She believes in the importance of giving back to our communities, although she is quick to qualify that term by saying, "There is a huge misconception about what that means." As she beautifully states, "One doesn't need to have a big bank account. One can give back through compassion, empathy, forgiveness, kindness, and love."

Journalist and former Ebert Fellow Tiffany Walden won the Racial Equity in Journalism grant from Borealis Philanthropy and finds empathy to be a driving force in her company's mission to help reshape narratives as they tell the stories of Black

Chicagoans. They have recently published stories uplifting the voices of inmates and their families who worry about safety while incarcerated in Illinois correctional facilities and the voices of tenants and landlords affected by the pandemic. Tiffany also actively encourages her fellow reporters to apply empathy and compassion when interviewing the community.

Ebert Fellow and University of Illinois grad Hal Burgan regularly allows empathy to lead his work and studies in film, creative writing, and philosophy. When he sits down to edit or provide feedback, he finds himself reminded of an interview with Albert Maysles. When Maysles was asked how he ensures that he delivers authentic portrayals of his documentaries' subjects, he said that it was fairly easy. All he had to do was approach the subject with empathy. Burgan has come to believe that to get the most out of the act of editing, the editor must approach the author and the work itself "with empathy at the forefront of their mind." He also believes that different ways of storytelling further empathetic editing, and he has realized that encountering more of others' work during the editing process has helped open him up to that which lies beyond his particular style. Burgan reminds us that we can all act with empathy in whatever creative endeavors we pursue.

Aspiring film and television producer, screenwriter, and Ebert Fellow Coltrane Zerai-Che has followed a similar trajectory. She says she will always base her creative ideas off of forgiveness, empathy, compassion, and kindness. Filmmaker and editor Brandon Towns also chooses to extend an attitude of empathy and compassion with his volunteer work helping a local chapter of the National Association for the Advancement of Colored People (NAACP) create awareness of the organization's reemergence on campus at Bradley University. He has collaborated with local POC (people of color) filmmakers to tell empathic stories about marginalized groups and specifically supports people with anxiety, having suffered from it himself. The transformations witnessed with each fellow warmed my heart. The same was true of fellow Joshua Lee when he moved from Oahu, Hawaii, to Burbank, California, to shoot a Netflix film. When he shared thoughts about his early projects, he said that before he was on a path of doing creative work only for himself, but he then realized the importance of reaching out to other people.

The FECK principles are boundless, giving us the opportunity to integrate them into every aspect of our lives—professional or personal, individual or global.

Many of our Ebert Fellows have extended the FECK principles not only into their work but also into their daily lives. When the COVID-19 pandemic hit, former Ebert Fellow Laura Garber went from traveling the world, riding on the back of a dusty motorbike through green Vietnam villages, to being quarantined at home with her mom. Coming back together was an adjustment for both of them, as they navigated the occasional misunderstanding or instances when they felt either blame or lack of acceptance. Laura thought about a saying she once heard, "Children never forgive their mothers," and chose to make an effort to understand her mother's sacrifices and gifts better. She found a list of films that best portrayed their relationship as mother and daughter, and they agreed upon the 1983 film *Terms of Endearment* as the winner. Watching it together, they saw their relationship in Shirley MacLaine's character, Aurora, and Debra Winger's Emma. They had faults but were lovable. Out of stubbornness, Laura refused to cry in front of her mom during any of the scenes. Yet a few days later, as she lay on a freshly mown lawn, under the first sun of the week, she found herself no longer immune to empathy and compassion and gave way to her emotions. She said the tears came when she thought about the movie's scene in which Emma's preteen boy comes to visit her for the final time in the hospital. Her son pretends to be cold, as if he doesn't care. Despite the standoffish attitude he exhibited toward her, Debra Winger's character connects with him naturally, and in a nurturing, motherly way. She tells him, "I know you've always loved me," then adds that if he were to feel guilty for being detached later, "don't." Just like the characters in the movie, Laura found herself filled with gratitude for her mother's forgiveness and compassion.

Emma Piper-Burket recognized the power of community and collaboration during the pandemic. In her words, "It's something I've been cultivating in small ways, such as putting a vegetable garden in my front yard at my house in Detroit, rather than the backyard." Her garden became a way to share experiences with neighbors and passersby. People have asked her to help them build garden beds to grow their own food, and neighbors' children have come over to help plant seeds and water the plants. Those driving by will stop and share in conversations about the power of growing our own food and in that small action, Emma found great power during uncertain times. Also helping her community was Ebert Fellow Mariah Schaefer, who initiated a "zero waste" practice in her life to show empathy for the planet. In her words, "When we show empathy, kindness, and compassion to our planet, everyone benefits. Sometimes we get so caught up with our problems and responsibilities that we forget to observe how much goodness there is in the world."

Forgiveness lays the foundation for us to be more empathetic, compassionate, and kind. Empathy allows us to deeply understand and relate to others. Compassion leads us to want to help alleviate the suffering and lift the spirits of others, so they can fulfill their destinies. Kindness, then, becomes about the simple acts that spur forgiveness, empathy, and compassion into action.

Kindness is critical in creating a global community that gives a FECK. I am so grateful to those who had the vision and generosity to help bring the Roger Ebert Center to fruition for the students and the town's people alike, and I look forward to the fruits of what is being seeded. What we all sow within our youth and young adults will continue to flourish as they grow into full-fledged adults. I believe this holds true for all four of the FECK principles. Forgiveness is freeing ourselves to love; empathy is emotionally relating to others; and compassion is about listening deeply to understand other people's challenges, ease their suffering, and lift their spirits; kindness, then, is that next step where you say, "This is what I can do," and then you actually do it. Kindness also helps foster even deeper levels of compassion and it helps us to be more forgiving. Kindness is the knot that ties all the FECK principles together, propelling them into action and creating an enduring impact.

On the following pages, you will find exercises you can undertake to help build your kindness muscle and questions that will help you contemplate the formal and informal ways you can give your time, yourself, and your heart every day. I hope they help you open yourself up to the wonder of humanity.

Kindness Journal

Opportunities for kindness are found when we choose to cast a loving, caring eye upon every person we meet or in every situation we encounter. Kindness can also be fostered through a little research, conversation, or inquiry to help identify a group in need, just as Candice Payne did during that bitterly cold winter in Chicago.

Kindness Exercise 1: Who Is in Need of Our Support?

Take time to think about or read the news headlines in your local community, then consider the following questions.

Who are the people or groups that are currently in need of additional support? ______________________

What are the ways in which I feel these people or groups could be best supported? ______________________

What simple acts of kindness could I contribute to this person or group? ______________________

What would I do if I were able to get very creative with my kindness? ______________________

What Will We Create in the World?

IF, IN THE PAST, I had stood on a street corner and shouted out how forgiveness, empathy, compassion, and kindness can lead to greater love and unity, people would have likely done one of three things: they would have walked by and smiled; they would have run past me quickly (thinking I had lost my mind); or, worse, they would have simply ignored me. But while it felt as though the COVID-19 pandemic shrank our world in many ways, it also helped to expand our thinking about what is possible when we unite in the name of hope and love. Today, I believe that we are shifting, that we are awakening to different ways of being, and that actions of forgiveness, empathy, compassion, and kindness are becoming more publicized and normalized. We are realizing that there is so much we can accomplish by contributing good in the world—to ourselves, to our neighbors, to our communities, and to our global society.

Sometimes the smallest actions have the greatest impact—like the ones we engage in when we think no one is watching. We don't need to have a lot or give a lot to do a lot for others. Conscientiousness and creativity go a long way, and every contribution matters. Candice Payne wasn't famous. She earned an average salary, but she was big in her thinking about how she could help homeless people during a polar vortex. Look at the impact of her one kind thought: she helped to save more than one hundred lives in a single night! California art teacher Mary Beth Heffernan had a simple vision: to help ease the anxieties of patients with Ebola by giving a face to the Liberian health-care workers who attended to them. She fought to find a partner to help bring her vision to life and didn't stop until she did. One could say her efforts lent comfort and brought smiles to the faces of doctors and patients during a horrific health crisis. The Amish people of Nickel Mines found it in their hearts to forgive Charles Roberts, which was far more than mere money could ever have done to rebuild their community. Mamie Till-Mobley fueled the civil rights movement with her staunch determination to bring empathy and awareness to the realities of lynchings and specifically to the brutal murder of her son, Emmett Till. Dimitri Neonakis drew a heart in the air when he could not hug his fellow Nova Scotians in person.

What can we accomplish by embracing the FECK principles? From the world I grew up in on Chicago's West Side, I've learned that giving a FECK has to be about fulfilling the basics first. That means supporting local families with food to eat, a roof over their heads, streets that are safe to be on at any time of day or night, neighbors who watch out for one another, and an end to gun violence and deaths. It means increasing the amount of hope our young people have for the future. I believe that working toward the goals the FECK principles represent will unquestionably lead to a world where

- we see less war and more peace;
- we see an increased emphasis on improving climate conditions and our air and water quality (because we understand that this

affects us globally and that we're all in this together);

- we see an increased emphasis on financial sustainability (this would not be a redistribution of wealth but rather the opportunity for each of us to support our whole family);
- we see an increased emphasis on medical *care* for all;
- we see an improvement in overall mental health;
- we see a decreased need for long-term imprisonment; and
- we see an uptick in our happiness quotient.

Our contributions in the name of empathy, compassion, and kindness can be big or small and made in whatever way is true to who we are.

This is *my* list. Each person has a different vision of the world, so I encourage you to compile your own list. As you have seen in the stories within this book, the four FECK principles have real-world consequences, especially when they are implemented every day. We don't need tragedy or challenges to motivate us to care; when we speak about having the ability to make a FECK contribution, we are talking about *everyone* being able to do so. Contributions are not contingent on race, age, gender, economic status, political or religious belief, geographic location, or even the size or scope of our efforts. Any one of the FECK capacities can be developed with intention. It is my hope that after reading the inspiring accounts in this book and practicing the tips provided, we can all step into the place of seeing ourselves as someone who cares enough to be forgiving, empathic, compassionate, and kind. No matter what side of the political spectrum you fall on, there exists an obvious need to unify humanity at this point in history. As I cannot emphasize enough, you also don't have to have an abundance of time or money.

Every one of us has the ability to affect

another in a positive way simply by acting out of forgiveness, empathy, compassion, and kindness. There is universality and all-around applicability to each of these four domains. It's important to note, however, that while the FECK principles outlined herein can be adopted and developed by any of us, this *isn't* a book about giving up our unique identities and becoming someone else to fit into a community. It's very much about bringing our individuality and our unique contributions to the whole of our communities. When we allow ourselves to be creative and individual in our acts of forgiveness, empathy, compassion, and kindness, we multiply the impact they have on those who need them. Our unique thoughts shape the actions that can bring a lightheartedness or smile to people experiencing even the most challenging times. They bring new perspective and growth to a situation that can feel difficult to move beyond. It's up to each of us to get creative about how we care, about how we challenge ourselves to think bigger about our contributions, and to *give a FECK* in every possible way we can.

Forgiveness, empathy, compassion, and kindness begin with being grounded in who you are, because it is from there that a true heart and impact can be felt.

When it comes to figuring out how we each want to contribute in the name of forgiveness, empathy, compassion, and kindness, we simply need to look inside ourselves for answers and inspired ideas. Know thyself first and go by your own moral compass. Do what is true to you. Take the stories and strategies inside these pages and adapt them to your life, your beliefs, and your own personal style. We don't necessarily need to seek input from an external source, because we have within us everything we need to make a difference! All we need is somewhere to start, some small action to take. When we have somewhere to start, creating a community and a world of greater love and unity becomes just a little less far-fetched. As Roger once said, "We must try to contribute joy to the world. That is true no matter what our problems, our health, our circumstances." Before he made his transition, he said that he was happy he lived long enough to find out that contributing joy and kindness is the best thing to do with a life. It is my wish that you may also find the "best things" to do with your life.

My FECK

HOW DO WE BEGIN today to be more forgiving, empathetic, compassionate, and kind? A few years ago, I came up with a concept I thought would have an unprecedented impact on our society. I wondered if it was too idealistic, so I didn't discuss it with many people at first. The idea centered around contributing 30 percent (#30percent). I thought that it would be great if we could change our laws to allow politicians to use 30 percent of their campaign funds to solve real-world problems. I read that one aspect of the Flint, Michigan, lead-poisoned water crisis could be resolved with $56 million and countered that point with the fact that hundreds of millions of dollars were being spent on presidential campaigns. If each of the national politicians, whether Republican or Democrat, put 30 percent of their monies into an aggregate fund, the general population could vote (via social media) on where the funds should be used.

The politicians and their constituents could then decide where to put their funds so we could elect a candidate based on their deeds as well their words. It seems like a much better use of the money than the obscene amounts that candidates spend on ads that attack their opponents. I would love for this proposal to be adopted.

I also had the vision of creating a National Department of Peace. We have a Department of Defense to assure our national security, especially during times of war, but what about a department where people are devoted to finding as many avenues of peace and harmony as our creative and diplomatic minds can muster? There are various units spread throughout our government that contain the seeds of something like this, but why not create a moonshot with the goal of decreasing violence and aggression and preserving peace in our communities, in our society, in our country, and in our world? Alongside the many examples of small ways we can act to create goodness, I wanted to share these two big national ideas with you to illustrate the momentum and potential that exists when we work together using the FECK principles.

The question that remains is this: What will be your creative way of applying the FECK principles? On the following pages, I invite you to create your own personal FECK manifesto. This is your opportunity to outline ideas for how you can contribute to the world when you lead with forgiveness, empathy, compassion, and kindness. If we all choose to give a FECK today, perhaps love can indeed affect our lives, save lives, and even survive death.

I do give a FECK! I am creative, caring, and kind. I foster forgiveness, empathy, compassion, and kindness in my thoughts, conversations, and actions. With the FECK principles in mind and heart, here are some things, big and small, that I can contribute to a person or group, locally or globally, to have a positive impact today.

FECK Contribution 1: ______________________

____

____

____

____

____

____

FECK Contribution 2: ______________________

____

____

____

____

____

____

FECK Contribution 3: ______________________

____

____

____

____

____

____

FECK Contribution 4: ______________________

____

____

____

____

____

____

FECK Contribution 5: ______________________

____

____

____

____

____

____

My ultimate FECK contribution will be:

____

____

____

____

____

____

____

About the Author

CHAZ EBERT is the CEO of Ebert Digital LLC, publisher of the preeminent movie review site RogerEbert.com. She is also a legal adviser and television and movie producer at Ebert Productions. For twenty-four years, she shared a life with Pulitzer Prize winner Roger Ebert. In their work to foster empathy through cinema and around the globe, they established the Ebertfest Film Festival and the Roger Ebert Center for Film Studies at the University of Illinois. Chaz has passionately continued to lead all established events, while endeavoring to nurture the next generation of film journalists, critics, filmmakers, and technologists through the Roger Ebert Fellowship, launched in 2014 by Sundance Institute founder Robert Redford, and the year-round Roger Ebert Fellowship program established at the University of Illinois at Urbana-Champaign in the College of Media. She also continues to award the Golden Thumb and Ebert Humanitarian Awards at Ebertfest and at the Toronto and Chicago International Film Festivals to filmmakers who exhibit an unusually compassionate view of the world.

As president of the Roger and Chaz Ebert Foundation, Chaz's civic passions include programs to help break the glass ceiling for women and people of color and to provide education and arts for women, children, and families. As the founder of "#Day4Empathy," Chaz has become celebrated in the media and Chicago community for spearheading efforts for kindness-induced change. In her pledge to foster the FECK principles of forgiveness, empathy, compassion, and kindness, she has also become a sought-out lecturer who has touched tens of thousands of attendees at events such as Cannes; Telluride Film Festival; the Palm Springs Film Festival; Toronto, Chicago, and Hawaii International Film Festivals; and the University of Illinois at Urbana-Champaign. Her contributions have garnered her the 2022 FACETS Legend Award, the 2022 Ruby Dee

Humanitarian award at the Black Reel Awards, and the 2011 Focus Achievement Award from Women in Film Chicago.

Previously an attorney, Chaz was named Lawyer of the Year by the Constitutional Rights Foundation. She was named the 2019 Beethoven Laureate for being "a humanist who promotes justice and a better world through the arts" by the International Beethoven Project. She currently acts as a life trustee of the Art Institute and serves on the boards of the Lyric Opera, the LA Opera, the Lincoln Presidential Foundation, After School Matters, the Shirley Ryan AbilityLab, FACETS Multimedia, and the Honorary Board of Family Focus. She has also served on the Lawyers Committees of the presidential campaigns for President Clinton, President Obama, and Senator Hillary Clinton.

Initiatives and Organizations

Ebertfest Film Festival

In 1998 we founded the annual film festival, originally called the Roger Ebert Overlooked Film Festival, at the University of Illinois in Champaign, Illinois. The name was changed to Roger Ebert's Film Festival, but it is more commonly referred to as Ebertfest. The mission is to bring people together under the best possible conditions to watch good cinema. The films chosen, whether domestic or foreign, result in an understanding of other peoples, other cultures, and others in circumstances different from our own, with the core principles of forgiveness, empathy, compassion, and kindness being woven into the fabric.

The films at the festival are screened one at a time, so everyone views the same film at the same time, promoting a strong sense of community among audience members, filmmakers, guests, students, and scholars.

Over the years, Ebertfest has evolved into a place to celebrate not only cinema but the very best in human nature. We give humanitarian awards to filmmakers who exhibit extraordinary empathic or compassionate views of the world. We established the Icon Award and have held academic panels that included in-depth discussions on eradicating the stigma of addiction and mental and physical disabilities through the arts.

The Roger Ebert Center, University of Illinois, College of Media, and the Ebert Symposium

We endowed an initial fund to establish the Roger Ebert Center for Film Studies at the University of Illinois in the College of Media in Champaign, Illinois. Since then, generous donors have contributed enough to make the Center a reality. This is Roger's alma mater, and he was so grateful for the education he received there. The purpose and the mission of the Center is to educate and inspire emerging writers, film critics, artists, filmmakers, and technologists to tell stories that matter, whether on-screen or through a variety of other forums.

While the center was in formation, we held the Ebert Symposium as public event seminars in an academic setting to exchange ideas about inclusion and diversity in a manner that could lead to active change. The symposium was designed to encourage ideas and acts that have immediate benefits for society, involving those who may be in a position to help create a more inclusive ecosystem.

Ebert Fellowship

We also support those whom we call our Ebert Fellows—emerging filmmakers, film critics, writers, and technologists—with grants and mentoring, in the hopes that they go on to create substantive films, start-up companies, and other means of spreading and encouraging empathy. The vision has always been that our fellows become ambassadors of compassion who venture out into the world and awaken others to the bigger-than-life feelings Roger thought were possible through empathy.

The Roger and Chaz Ebert Foundation

Through the Roger and Chaz Ebert Foundation, grants are awarded to organizations or individuals who work to improve the lives of others or advance humankind through the arts. Our primary focus is on women, children, and families.

#Day4Empathy

The April 4 #Day4Empathy serves as a call to action for more of the good in each of us to show up in our everyday interactions with other people in our work, study, and play. The event is about creating a better community and drawing each of us closer to our own best selves in our interactions with others. It's about having watercooler conversations about what empathy means to us while encouraging random acts of kindness.

Endnotes

1. "Lincoln Leadership Prize," Lincoln Presidential Foundation, accessed October 31, 2023, https://www.lincolnpresidential.org/giving/lincoln-leadership-prize/; Steven Spearie, "Remembering Tutu: Retired Archbishop Called Visit to Lincoln Presidential Library 'Moving,'" December 27, 2021, www.sj-r.com/story/news/2021/12/27/remembering-desmond-tutus-visit-lincoln-presidential-library-2008/9020512002/.

2. "The Emancipation Proclamation," National Archives, accessed October 31, 2023, www.archives.gov/exhibits/featured-documents/emancipation-proclamation.

3. "The Truth and Reconciliation Commission (TRC)," Apartheid Museum, accessed October 31, 2023, www.apartheidmuseum.org/exhibitions/the-truth-and-reconciliation-commission-trc.

4. "I Am Prepared to Die," Nelson Mandela Foundation, April 20, 2011, https://www.nelsonmandela.org/news/entry/i-am-prepared-to-die.

5. The sayings "Resentment is like swallowing poison and expecting the other person to die" and "Resentment is like drinking poison and hoping it will kill someone else" have been attributed to various sources, dating back decades. They continue to be referenced by groups such as Alcoholics Anonymous (AA).

6. Stacey E. McElroy et al., "Descriptions, Psychometric Support, and Recommendations for Research and Practice," in *Handbook of Forgiveness*, 2nd ed., eds. Everett L. Worthington Jr. and Nathaniel G. Wade (New York: Routledge, 2020), 74.

7. Fred Luskin, "What Is Forgiveness?," Institute of Noetic Sciences, September 15, 2009, YouTube video, www.youtube.com/watch?v=66Yxs1C_iQo.

8. "Charleston Shooting Survivors Open Up about the Power of Forgiveness," *TODAY*, September 20, 2018, YouTube video, www.youtube.com/watch?v=XdSLp4MmDRM.

9. Suzanne Freedman and Eva Yi-Ju Chen, "Forgiveness Education as a Form of Peace Education with Fifth-Grade Students: A Pilot Study with Implications for Educators," *Peace and Conflict: Journal of Peace Psychology 29, no.* 3 (2023): 235–46, doi.org/10.1037/pac0000676.

10. Geeta Ahirwar, Gyanesh Kumar Tiwari, and Pramod Kumar Rai, "Exploring the Nature, Attributes and Consequences of Forgiveness in Children: A Qualitative Study," *Psychological Thought* 12, no 2 (December 9, 2019): 214–31, https://doi.org/10.5964/psyct.v12i2.347.

11. Fred Luskin, "What Is Forgiveness?," Institute of Noetic Sciences, September 15, 2009, YouTube video, www.youtube.com/watch?v=66Yxs1C_iQo.

12. "Gunman Kills Five Students at Amish School," History.com, last updated September 30, 2020, www.history.com/this-day-in-history/gunman-kills-five-students-at-amish-school.

13. "Police: School Killer Told Wife He Molested Family Members," CNN, October 3, 2006, www.cnn.com/2006/US/10/03/amish.shooting/.

14. The Associated Press, "School shooter's wife thanks Amish community," NBC News, October 15, 2006. www.nbcnews.com/id/wbna15266663

15. Brandon J. Griffin et al., "Evaluating the Effectiveness of a Community-Based Forgiveness Campaign," *Journal of Positive Psychology* 14, no. 3 (February 28, 2018): 354–61, doi.org/10.1080/17439760.2018.1437464.

16. Joanna Walters, "'The Happening': 10 Years after the Amish Shooting," NPR, October 2, 2016, www.theguardian.com/us-news/2016/oct/02/amish-shooting-10-year-anniversary-pennsylvania-the-happening.

17. "Amish School Shooting," CBS News, October 2, 2006, www.cbsnews.com/pictures/amish-school-shooting/.

18. "New Schoolhouse Opens Near Site of Massacre," NBC News, April 2, 2007, www.nbcnews.com/id/wbna17911456.

19. Ben Lear, "They Call Us Monsters," January 20, 2017, https://www.youtube.com/watch?v=un8Uwg6SWG0

20. "Juan and Jarad Write from Prison," *Independent Lens,* PBS, May 17, 2017, www.pbs.org/independentlens/blog/juan-jarad-they-call-us-monsters-send-update-letter/.

21. "Juan and Jarad Write from Prison."

22. Martha Minow, "How Forgiveness Can Create a More Just Legal System," TEDWomen 2019, December 2019, video, www.ted.com

/talks/martha_minow_how_forgiveness_can_create_a_more_just _legal_system?language=en.

23. "The Drug War, Mass Incarceration and Race," Drug Policy Alliance, June 2015, www.unodc.org/documents/ungass2016/Contributions /Civil/DrugPolicyAlliance/DPA_Fact_Sheet_Drug_War_Mass _Incarceration_and_Race_June2015.pdf.

24. Minow, "Forgiveness."

25. Lydia Woodyatt et al., "Orientation to the Psychology of Self-Forgiveness," in *Handbook of the Psychology of Self-Forgiveness*, ed. Lydia Woodyatt et al. (New York: Springer, 2017): 6, doi.org/10.1002/cpp.2372.

26. Seonaid Cleare, Andrew Gumley, and Rory C. O'Connor; "Self-Compassion, Self-Forgiveness, Suicidal Ideation, and Self-Harm: A Systematic Review," *Clinical Psychology and Psychotherapy* 26, no. 5 (October 22, 2019): 511-30, doi.org/10.1002/cpp.2372.

27. "Fact Check: Courts Have Dismissed Multiple Lawsuits of Alleged Electoral Fraud Presented by Trump Campaign," Reuters, February 15, 2021, www.reuters.com/article/uk-factcheck-courts-election-idUSKB-N2AF1G1.

28. Chaz Ebert, "Disturbing the Peace: Stephen Apkon Talks to Chaz Ebert," RogerEbert.com, November 8, 2016, www.rogerebert.com/chazs-blog/disturbing-the-peace-stephen-apkon-talks-to-chaz-ebert.

29. Lauren Kirchner, "The Psychology and Biology of Road Rage," *Pacific Standard*, last updated June 14, 2017, psmag.com/social-justice /psychology-biology-road-rage-73416.

30. Jamil Zaki and Mina Cikara, "Addressing Empathic Failures," *Current Directions in Psychological Science* 24, no. 6 (December 10, 2015): 471–76, doi.org/10.1177/0963721415599978.

31. Christine Cong Guo, "The Neuroscience of Empathy," in *The Routledge Handbook of Philosophy of Empathy*, ed. Heidi L. Maibom (New York: Routledge, 2017), 44.

32. Heidi L. Maibom, "Affective Empathy," in *The Routledge Handbook of Philosophy of Empathy*, ed. Heidi L. Maibom (New York: Routledge, 2017), 22–23.

33. Roger Ebert, "A Day of Loss and Passage," rogerebert.com, March 8, 2011 www.rogerebert.com/reviews/i-will-follow-2011.

34. Odie Henderson, "Selma," RogerEbert.com, December 24, 2014, www.rogerebert.com/reviews/selma-2014.

35. "Roger Ebert on Empathy," RogerEbert.com, April 04, 2018, video, www.rogerebert.com/empathy/video-roger-ebert-on-empathy.

36. "Emmett Till Is Murdered," This Day in History: August 28, History.com, accessed November 5, 2023, www.history.com/this-day-in-history/the-death-of-emmett-till.

37. Grace Hauck, "'Let the World See': Church Where 100,000 Saw Emmett Till's Open Casket Is Now on a List of US Endangered Historic Places," *USA Today*, last updated September 25, 2020, www.usatoday.com/story/news/nation/2020/09/24/chicago-church-where-emmett-tills-viewing-drew-thousands-endangered/3522968001/.

38. "The Trial of J. W. Milam and Roy Bryant," PBS, accessed November 6, 2023, www.pbs.org/wgbh/americanexperience/features/emmett-trial-jw-milam-and-roy-bryant/.

39. "Emmett Till Murderers Make Magazine Confession," This Day in History: January 24, History.com, www.history.com/this-day-in-history/emmett-till-murderers-make-magazine-confession.

40. "The Bus Boycott," Library of Congress, accessed November 6, 2023, www.loc.gov/exhibitions/rosa-parks-in-her-own-words/about-this-exhibition/the-bus-boycott/emmett-till-with-his-mother/.

41. "H.R. 55—Emmett Till Antilynching Act," 117th Cong. (2022), www.congress.gov/bill/117th-congress/house-bill/55.

42. Charles Darwin, *The Descent of Man* (London: John Murray, 1879; New York: Penguin, 2004), 147.

43. Darwin, *Descent of Man,* 130.

44. Darwin, *Descent of Man,* 147.

45. John Paul Rollert, "Reversed on Appeal: The Uncertain Future of President Obama's 'Empathy Standard,'" *Yale Law Journal,* October 15, 2010, www.yalelawjournal.org/forum/reversed-on-appeal-the-uncertain-future-of-president-obamas-qempathy-standardq.

46. Jamil Zaki and Mina Cikara, "Addressing Empathic Failures," *Current Directions in Psychological Science* 24, no. 6 (December 10, 2015): 471–76, doi.org/10.1177/0963721415599978.

47. Deborah Day, "Shonda Rhimes Really Hates the Word 'Diversity': 'I'm Normalizing TV,' The Wrap, March 16, 2015, www.thewrap.com/shonda-rhimes-really-hates-the-word-diversity-im-normalizing-tv/.

48. Nicholas Bogel-Burroughs, "Prosecutors Say Derek Chauvin Knelt on George Floyd for 9 Minutes 29 Seconds, Longer Than Initially Reported,"

New York Times, March 30, 2021, www.nytimes.com/2021/03/30/us/derek-chauvin-george-floyd-kneel-9-minutes-29-seconds.html?smid=url-share.

49. Lily Rothman, "What Martin Luther King Jr Really Thought about Riots," *TIME*, April 28, 2015, time.com/3838515/baltimore-riots-language-unheard-quote/.

50. "The 1619 Project," *New York Times Magazine*, August 16, 2019, www.nytimes.com/interactive/2019/08/14/magazine/1619-america-slavery.html.

51. Elana Lyn Gross, "Trump Signs Executive Order to Establish a 1776 Commission to Instill 'Patriotic Education,'" *Forbes*, November 2, 2020, www.forbes.com/sites/elanagross/2020/11/02/trump-signs-executive-order-to-establish-a-1776-commission-to-instill-patriotic-education/?sh=26ffd76b6dc3.

52. "Governor Ron DeSantis Signs Legislation to Protect Floridians from Discrimination and Woke Indoctrination," Government of Florida, *April 22, 2022,* https://www.flgov.com/2022/04/22/governor-ron-desantis-signs-legislation-to-protect-floridians-from-discrimination-and-woke-indoctrination/.

53. Gabrielle Chung, "NASCAR Driver Bubba Wallace Pushes for Removal of Confederate Flags at Race Tracks," *People*, June 9, 2020, people.com/sports/nascar-driver-bubba-wallace-pushes-for-removal-of-confederate-flags-at-race-tracks/.

54. Steve Wyche, "Colin Kaepernick Explains Why He Sat during National Anthem," NFL, August 27, 2016, www.nfl.com/news/colin-kaepernick-explains-why-he-sat-during-national-anthem-0ap3000000691077.

55. Chloe Melas, "NFL Commissioner Roger Goodell Says League Was Wrong for Not Listening to Players Earlier about Racism," CNN, last updated June 6, 2020, www.cnn.com/2020/06/05/sport/roger-goodell-responds-nfl-stronger-together-video.

56. Roger Goodell, "Protesting the National Anthem—Episode 8," August 2020, in *Uncomfortable Conversations with Emmanuel Acho*, podcast, YouTube video, https://uncomfortableconvos.com/episode/episode-8.

57. A Mile in My Shoes, Empathy Museum, www.empathymuseum.com/a-mile-in-my-shoes/.

58. Roman Krznaric, "Six Habits of Highly Empathic People," Greater Good, Greater Good Science Center, University of California, Berkeley, November 27, 2012, greatergood.berkeley.edu/article/item/six_habits_of_highly_empathic_people1.

ENDNOTES

59. Sourya Acharya and Samarth Shukla, "Mirror neurons: Enigma of the metaphysical modular brain," National Library of Medicine, Jul-Dec 2012, www.ncbi.nlm.nih.gov/pmc/articles/PMC3510904/.

60. Jamil Zaki and Mina Cikara, "Addressing Empathic Failures," *Current Directions in Psychological Science* 24, no. 6 (December 10, 2015): 471–76, doi.org/10.1177/0963721415599978.

61. Zaki and Cikara, "Addressing Empathic Failures."

62. Zaki and Cikara, "Addressing Empathic Failures."

63. Mary Mazzio, "A Most Beautiful Thing: Director's Statement," RogerEbert.com, March 12, 2020, www.rogerebert.com/chazs-blog/a-most-beautiful-thing-directors-statement.

64. Mazzio, "Most Beautiful Thing."

65. Mazzio, "Most Beautiful Thing."

66. Tiffany Shlain is also the founder of two global initiatives: Character Day and 50/50 Day. Character Day explores the science of character, and 50/50 Day focuses on gender equity. The objective is to provide unified days of film and discussion about important issues shaping our lives by uniting over 100,000 live events. Character Day so far brought together over 200,000 groups in 125 countries and all 50 states, for a total of 15,000 schools and over 4 million people.

67. "The Adaptable Mind," Tiffany Shlain & Let It Ripple Studio, October 8, 2015, YouTube video, www.youtube.com/watch?v=937iCwJd3fI.

68. Andrew Johnson, "Health Care Worker Covered in Protective Gear Laminates Smile on Chest to Comfort Patients," NBC San Diego, April 6, 2020, www.nbcsandiego.com/news/local/health-care-worker-covered-in-protective-gear-laminates-smile-on-chest-to-comfort-patients/2300695/.

69. Emma Seppälä, "The Power & Science of Social Connection," TEDx Talks, April 1, 2014, YouTube video, youtu.be/WZvUppaDfNs?si=4TWVQ7TGISDIQxJp.

70. "The Empathy Exams," Graywolf Press, accessed November 6, 2023, www.graywolfpress.org/books/empathy-exams.

71. Emma Pattee, "5 People Who Can Help You Strengthen Your Empathy Muscle," *New York Times*, October 4, 2020, www.nytimes.com/2020/10/04/smarter-living/5-people-who-can-help-you-strengthen-your-empathy-muscle.html.

72. Martin Luther King Jr., "MLK Speaks in Chicago," 1966, WGN TV,

April 4, 2018, Facebook video, https://www.facebook.com/WGNTV/videos/mlk-speaks-in-chicago/10155443360577411/.

73. Emma Seppälä, "The Compassionate Mind," Association for Psychological Science, April 30, 2013, https://www.psychologicalscience.org/observer/the-compassionate-mind.

74. Seppälä, "Compassionate Mind."

75. "Meet Robert S. Feder, MD, the 2023 Recipient of the Gary A. Mecklenburg Distinguished Physician Award," Northwestern Medicine, accessed November 2, 2023, https://jobs.nm.org/Meet-Robert-S-Feder-MD-the-2023-Recipient-of-the-Gary-A-Mecklenburg-Distinguished-Physician-Award.

76. Dr. Kristin Neff, "Definition of Self-Compassion," Self-Compassion.org, accessed November 6, 2023, https://self-compassion.org/the-three-elements-of-self-compassion-2/.

77. "What Is Self-Compassion," Center for Mindful Self-Compassion, accessed November 6, 2023, https://centerformsc.org/learn-msc/.

78. Neff, "Definition of Self-Compassion."

79. Amy Berish, "FDR and Polio," Franklin D. Roosevelt Presidential Library and Museum, accessed November 6, 2023, www.fdrlibrary.org/polio.

80. John Boyko, "2020 Nova Scotia Attacks," *Canadian Encyclopedia*, April 15, 2021, www.thecanadianencyclopedia.ca/en/article/2020-nova-scotia-attacks.

81. "Newfoundlander in Nova Scotia 'Paying Back' Support He Received after His Own Tragedy," CBC News, April 21, 2020, www.cbc.ca/news/canada/newfoundland-labrador/dave-brown-portapique-nova-scotia-1.5539295

82. Nikitha Martins, "Pilot Flies over Nova Scotia Creating a Heart-Shape Path in Tribute to Mass Shooting Victims," CityTV News, April 21, 2020, https://vancouver.citynews.ca/2020/04/21/pilot-flies-nova-scotia-heart-tribute-mass-shooting-victims/.

83. Karen Armstrong, *Twelve Steps to a Compassionate Life* (New York: Borzoi, 2010), 19.

84. "What Is Compassion?," *Greater Good*, Greater Good Science Center, University of California, Berkeley, greatergood.berkeley.edu/topic/compassion/definition.

ENDNOTES

85. Clara Strauss et al., "What Is Compassion and How Can We Measure It? A Review of Definitions and Measures," *Clinical Psychology Review* 47 (May 2016): 15–27, www.researchgate.net/publication/303600556_What_is_Compassion_and_How_Can_We_Measure_it_A_Review_of_Definitions_and_Measures.

86. Love Beyond Walls home page, accessed November 6, 2023, www.lovebeyondwalls.org/.

87. Chris Lumsden and Will Linendoll, "Man Assembles Handwashing Stations for Homeless amid Coronavirus," *Good Morning America*, December 28, 2020, www.goodmorningamerica.com/living/story/man-assembles-handwashing-stations-homeless-amid-coronavirus-69747192.

88. Joanna Peplak and Tina Malti, "Toward Generalized Concern: The Development of Compassion and Links to Kind Orientations," *Journal of Adolescent Research* 37, no. 6 (2022): 777, https://journals.sagepub.com/doi/pdf/10.1177/07435584211007840.

89. Anna Lucas, "Cultivating Connection: A Conceptual Model Identifying Facilitating and Inhibiting Factors across Three Levels of Community" (master's thesis, University of Pennsylvania, 2019), 2, https://repository.upenn.edu/mapp_capstone/226/.

90. Lucas, "Cultivating Connection," 45–49.

91. Tyler Lauletta, "Bills and Bengals Fans Gathered at the Hospital Caring for Damar Hamlin and Shared a Moment of Prayer," Insider, January 3, 2023, www.insider.com/damar-hamlin-bills-bengals-fans-pray-hospital-2023-1.

92. Coral Smith, "Damar Hamlin Speaks Out for First Time Since Cardiac Arrest, Expresses Gratitude for Widespread Support," NFL, January 28, 2023, www.nfl.com/news/damar-hamlin-speaks-out-for-first-time-since-cardiac-arrest-expresses-gratitude-.

93. John Marshall, "NFL Honors: Hamlin Joins Medical Staff That Saved His Life," Associated Press, February 9, 2023, https://apnews.com/article/damar-hamlin-joins-medical-responders-nfl-awards-9c2556e28daa103854f7dbfc0a88b997.

94. Barbara L. Frederickson and Daniel J. Siegel, "Broaden-and-Build Theory Meets Interpersonal Neurobiology as a Lens on Compassion and Positivity Resonance," in *Compassion: Concepts, Research and Applications*, ed. Paul Gilbert (New York: Routledge, 2017), 203–4.

95. "Arlene Samen, APRN," . NYAGI, www.nyagi.org/arlene-samen

96. "Our Vision," One Heart Worldwide, accessed November 3, 2023, https://oneheartworldwide.org/our-mission.

97. To learn more about how One Heart Worldwide works to provide essential services to pregnant women and newborns, visit "Network of Safety," One Heart Worldwide, https://oneheartworldwide.org/network-of-safety.

98. Maudlyne Ihejirika, "Candice Payne: Viral Deed of Housing Homeless at Hotel 'Was a No-Brainer,'" *Chicago Sun-Times*, February 10, 2019, https://chicago.suntimes.com/2019/2/10/18413042/candice-payne-viral-deed-of-housing-homeless-at-hotel-was-a-no-brainer.

99. Candice Payne, "Ellen Meets Inspiring Woman Who Helped Homeless During Polar Vortex," *The Ellen Show,* February 6, 2019, YouTube video, www.youtube.com/watch?v=y9NQSHeRdAk.

100. Ihejirika, "Candice Payne."

101. 101 "Quotations of Mahatma Gandhi," Gandhi World, https://gandhi-world.in/english/quotesAction.html

102. Joanna Peplak and Tina Malti, "Toward Generalized Concern: The Development of Compassion and Links to Kind Orientations," *Journal of Adolescent Research* 37, no. 6 (2022): 779, https://journals.sagepub.com/doi/pdf/10.1177/07435584211007840.

103. Oliver Scott Curry et al., "Happy to Help? A Systematic Review and Meta-Analysis of the Effects of Performing Acts of Kindness on the Well-Being of the Actor," *Journal of Experimental Social Psychology* 76 (May 2018): 320–29, www.sciencedirect.com/science/article/pii/S0022103117303451.

104. Steve Hartman, "How a Cup of Coffee from a Gym Owner Changed a Homeless Man's Life," CBS News, June 9, 2023, www.cbsnews.com/news/how-a-cup-of-coffee-from-a-gym-owner-changed-a-homeless-mans-life/.

105. Philip Cook, Elaina Mack, and Manuel Manrique, "Protecting Young Children from Violence in Colombia: Linking Caregiver Empathy with Community Child Rights Indicators as a Pathway for Peace in Medellin's Comuna 13," Peace and Conflict: Journal of Peace Psychology 23, no. 1 (February 2017): 38–45, www.researchgate.net/publication/313541104_Protecting_young_children_from_violence_in_Colombia_Linking_caregiver_empathy_with_community_child_rights_indicators_as_a_pathway_for_peace_in_Medellin's_Comuna_13.

106. Joanna Peplak and Tina Malti, "Toward Generalized Concern: The

Development of Compassion and Links to Kind Orientations," *Journal of Adolescent Research* 37, no. 6 (2022): 776, https://journals.sagepub.com/doi/pdf/10.1177/07435584211007840.

107. Molly Oswaks, "Over 3 Million People Took This Course on Happiness. Here's What Some Learned," *New York Times*, March 13, 2021, www.nytimes.com/2021/03/13/style/happiness-course.html.

108. Erik Ofgang, "1.5 Million People Register Online for Free Yale Happiness Course in Wake of Coronavirus," *Connecticut Magazine*, CT Insider, April 15, 2020, www.ctinsider.com/connecticutmagazine/health/article/1-5-million-people-register-online-for-free-Yale-17045268.php.

109. John Donne, "No Man Is an Island," Mensa for Kids, accessed November 6, 2023, www.mensaforkids.org/read/a-year-of-living-poetically/donne-no-man-is-an-island/.

110. "James Harrison's Story," Australian Red Cross Lifeblood, www.lifeblood.com.au/news-and-stories/stories/james-harrison; Kate Spalding, "How James Harrison, the 'Man with the Golden Arm,' Saved Nearly 2.5 Million Babies' Lives," IFL Science, July 22, 2022, www.iflscience.com/how-james-harrison-the-man-with-the-golden-arm-saved-the-lives-of-nearly-2-5-million-babies-64554.

111. Spalding, "Man with the Golden Arm."

112. Spalding, "Man with the Golden Arm."

113. Spalding, "Man with the Golden Arm."

114. "James Harrison's Story."

115. Martin Dufwenberg and Georg Kirchsteiger, "Modelling Kindness," *Journal of Economic Behavior & Organization* 167 (March 2018): 228–34, www.sciencedirect.com/science/article/abs/pii/S0167268118301987.

116. Jack Zenger and Joseph Folkman, "The Trickle-Down Effect of Good (and Bad) Leadership," *Harvard Business Review*, January 14, 2016, hbr.org/2016/01/the-trickle-down-effect-of-good-and-bad-leadership.

117. Weiming Tang et al., "How Kindness Can Be Contagious in Healthcare," *Nature Medicine* 27 (June 14, 2021): 1142–44, www.nature.com/articles/s41591-021-01401-x.

118. Boğaçhan Çelen, Andrew Schotter, and Mariana Blanco, "On Blame and Reciprocity: Theory and Experiments," *Journal of Economic Theory* 169 (May 2017): 62–92, www.researchgate.net/publication/316608344_On_blame_and_reciprocity_Theory_and_experiments.

119. Tang, "Kindness Can Be Contagious."

120. Tang, "Kindness Can Be Contagious."

121. "A Bit More About Us," Kindness Factory, https://kindnessfactory.com/about/.

122. "A Bit More About Us."

123. "About Kindness Factory," Kindness Factory, accessed November 6, 2023, https://kindnessfactory.com/about/, used with permission; Kindness Curriculum home page, accessed November 6, 2023, https://thekindnesscurriculum.com/, used with permission.

124. "About Kindness Factory."

125. Bryant P. H. Hui et al., "Rewards of Kindness? A Meta-Analysis of the Link between Prosociality and Well-Being," *Psychological Bulletin* 146, no. 12 (December 2020): 1084–1116, pubmed.ncbi.nlm.nih.gov/32881540/.

126. "*Come from Away*: The True Story," *Come from Away* official tour website, accessed November 6, 2023, https://comefromaway.com/story.php.

127. "*Come from Away*: The True Story."

128. Jackie Cooperman, "Meet the Canadians Who Opened Their Doors to Stranded Travelers after 9/11," *New York Post*, February 26, 2017, https://nypost.com/2017/02/26/meet-the-canadians-who-opened-their-doors-to-stranded-travelers-after-911/; Margarita Maltceva, "Unga, the Bonobo Ape Stranded in Canada after 9/11 Attacks, Dies at the Age of 29," *National Post*, March 17, 2021, https://nationalpost.com/news/world/unga-the-bonobo-ape-stranded-in-canada-after-9-11-attacks-dies-at-the-age-of-29.

129. Kayley Bayne and Dan Witters, "Saying Hello Linked to Higher Wellbeing, but with Limits," Gallup, August 15, 2023, https://news.gallup.com/poll/509543/saying-hello-linked-higher-wellbeing-limits.aspx.